# Power Retail

## Winning Strategies from Chapters and other Leading Retailers in Canada

# Power Retail

---

## Winning Strategies from Chapters and other Leading Retailers in Canada

---

LAWRENCE N. STEVENSON

JOSEPH C. SHLESINGER ✦ MICHAEL R. PEARCE

McGraw-Hill
Ryerson

Toronto  Montréal  New York  Burr Ridge  Bangkok  Bogotá  Caracas
Lisbon  London  Madrid  Mexico City  Milan  New Delhi  Seoul
Singapore  Sydney  Taipei

**McGraw-Hill
Ryerson Limited**
A Subsidiary of The **McGraw·Hill** Companies

ISBN: 0-07-560996-7

1234567890 TRI 99
Printed and bound in Canada.

**Canadian Cataloguing in Publication Data**

Stevenson, Lawrence N.
    Power retail: winning strategies from Chapters and other leading retailers
    in Canada

Includes index.

ISBN 0-07-560996-7

1. Retail trade – Management.  2. Retail trade – Canada – Management.
3. Retail trade – United States – Management.  I. Title.

HF5429.6.C3S73   1999      658.8'7'00971      C99-932103-X

Publisher: **Joan Homewood**
Editorial Co-ordinator: **Catherine Leek**
Production Co-ordinator: **Susanne Penny**
Editor: **Lynn Schellenberg**
Electronic Page Design and Composition: **Heidy Lawrance Associates**
Cover Design: **Art Plus**

# Table of Contents

# Introduction

*Power Retail* is about winning in retailing. In writing this book, we set out to explore a vital question: why do some retail firms do so well (the ones we call "power retailers"), while others do not? In other words, why has the retail industry become polarized between the power retailers at the top and those barely getting by; between those chalking up financial gains and exceptional stock performance and those struggling to keep their doors open? Retailers are all playing in the same market yet the performance gap between the top players and the rest clearly continues to widen. The results of our exploration are set out in this book, a book intended primarily for those who lead, and those who aspire to lead, retail organizations. We hope others who are interested in the retail business will also gain from our analysis and insights.

There are many good books and articles on business management, but few directly devoted to retailing, and virtually none about retail strategy. If it were as simple as "location, location, location" there would be no need for this book.

We believe that there are enough unique characteristics about retailing to merit detailed attention to how winners succeed and, of course, what the rest of us might learn from those successes – so we wrote this book. Within these covers we have mapped the strategies that drove retail success, and while we know better than to promise that there is one simple formula, it isn't rocket science either.

The author team brings a varied background and set of skills to the task. Larry Stevenson is CEO of Canada's leading book retail chain, Chapters. Joe Shlesinger is Managing Director of Bain & Company Canada, a strategic consulting firm. Michael Pearce is Associate Dean: Programs and Eaton/NSERC/SSCHRC Chair in Retailing at the Richard Ivey School of Business, The University of Western Ontario. Each of us has been actively involved in all facets of the retail industry for decades – as executives, investors, consultants, and researchers – so we decided to join forces to undertake this expedition.

We began by testing our observation that retail winners really do stand out from the pack in terms of their financial performance. We developed a performance indicator database of North American retailers. Using annual reports, Value Line, stock performance, and overall growth to create the database, we compared the financial performance of 226 of the largest North American retailers, representing more than $930 billion in sales each year. We were surprised at how dramatic the financial performance differences are between the retail winners and the rest of the pack. Accordingly, we decided to investigate the keys to retail success. The bulk of this book is an organized report of our analysis, observations and conclusions.

We were able to draw on more than our individual experiences to answer our question. Not only did we have access to seemingly unlimited information in university libraries and files, we also had access to Bain & Company's files (more than 400 retail assignments performed by Bain worldwide during the 1990s) and Chapters' own research studies. But perhaps most importantly, we undertook some original in-depth research with retail leaders. We surveyed 70 retail executives and personally interviewed two dozen key executives in retail firms operating in Canada. A distinctive "success pattern" emerged as we explored retail success (and retail failure). Once that pattern was clear to us, the structure of this book naturally followed.

The book is organized into nine chapters. In Chapter 1, we describe the current state of the retailing industry, our conception of power retailers, and our approach to discovering why

power retailers outperform the rest. We also outline the four principles of retail success that emerged from our work and provide
an overview of the remainder of the book.

The power retailers followed four principles:

- They deliver a customer-driven, superior Retail Value Propo-
sition (RVP).
- They lead geographic markets, categories, and channels.
- They execute better than competitors in the areas of people,
technology, and costs.
- They lead change by continually reinventing themselves.

The first principle, Retail Value Proposition (RVP), is explored
in Chapters 2 and 3. We discuss how power retailers segment
markets to select targets. In particular, we illustrate how needs-
based market segmentation provides better insights for retail market planning. In Chapter 3, we elaborate upon that concept and
illuminate the four major strategic ways to achieve competitive
advantage in value proposition.

The second principle is the topic of Chapter 4. Achieving dominance in geographic markets, product categories, and channels
is discussed along with concepts such as relative market share.

While the first two principles are oriented toward strategy for-
mulation, the third principle is about execution of strategy. We
found that executives put great emphasis on executional issues
so we deal with them in the next three chapters. Chapter 5 is
about getting the best from one's people. We share our findings
about retail leadership, management, motivation, and more. In
Chapter 6, we turn to technology and how it is reinventing retailing. As best we could, we stayed away from being too technical in
our discussion of retail information technology, focusing instead
on the enabling and transforming role that technology is playing in power retailing. In Chapter 7, the topic is cost management. In an industry with shrinking margins and rapid change
in structure, cost management is more critical than ever. The
tremendous success of discount formats illustrates how cost control can lead to a sustainable competitive advantage in retailing.

The fourth principle is all about change. The irony is that getting the RVP right, dominating the market, and executing well can lull a retail winner into a false sense of security. In an industry that is changing so rapidly that complacency is fatal, market share shifts are swift and frequent. In Chapter 8, we discuss the need for constant change and how power retailers make change happen. The reinvention of retailing that is now underway due to the Internet is also explored.

Chapter 9 is a summary, but with a twist. There is little doubt that Wal-Mart is a superb power retailer, so we examined that company from the perspective of our four principles, showing how its inspiring success can be explained by superior strategy, execution and constant change.

Throughout the book, we have provided numerous short examples of retailers who are doing something noteworthy in the area of power retailing. In addition to the short stories, we provide an ongoing, integrated example, the Chapters story, at the end of each chapter – after all, with the Chapters' founder as an author, we had access to all the data for this power retailer.

We believe retailing is an exciting profession and for those who do it well, highly rewarding. We hope this book invigorates your approach to retailing and contributes to your success.

Larry Stevenson
Joe Shlesinger
Michael Pearce

# 1

# Why Power Retailers Succeed Despite the Odds

*"A retail winner is as obvious to me as the nose on my face. It all comes down to strategy, to focus, to culture, to dedication. One can see it in The Gap. Their product is superior, their stores are superior, their people and their training are superior, you know where they are going. It's wonderful and exciting to see. The retail business may be one of the most difficult businesses in which to build sustainable advantage. Nothing is sacrosanct any more. The only way to succeed is to constantly ask 'How can I get better?'"*

— Elliott Wahle, President and CEO, Dylex

The power retailers are winning and they're winning big-time.

The retail winners like Wal-Mart, Home Depot, Loblaws, and Shoppers Drug Mart do more than just win. They significantly and consistently outperform the pack and win the hearts, and the wallets, of customers. While the power retailers report unprecedented increases in sales, others are going belly-up. While the powers double, even quadruple, their profits in a fiscal year, other retailers struggle to staunch the flow of red ink.

In recent years the retail industry has become polarized between winners and losers. As Figure 1.1 illustrates, over the last 10 years North American power retailers have managed to achieve truly spectacular stock price performance relative to their peers.

Why is there such a gulf between the power retailers at the top and those retailers barely getting by, between those chalking up financial gains and exceptional stock performance and those struggling just to keep their doors open? Retailers are all playing in the same market, yet the performance gap between the top players and the rest clearly continues to widen.

**FIGURE 1.1**

### Stock Price Performance of Publicly-Traded Retailers

A dollar invested in power retailers would be worth in excess of six dollars, compared to less than three for a retail index.

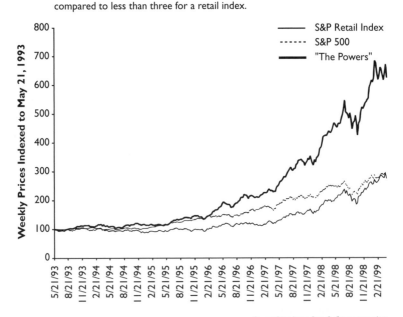

Source: Dow Jones, Bain & Company analysis

This question and our perceptions of today's dramatically changed retail landscape initiated our comprehensive study of the power retailers, a study that would culminate in the development of four clear principles for retail success. We believe that by adhering to these principles, any retailer – even those in low-growth markets – can be a winner.

## Changing Winds and Turbulent Waters

The retail environment of today has changed dramatically from that of the 1980s. The days of smooth sailing are long gone.

In the 1980s, who would have placed a bet that the venerable Eaton's chain would teeter on the verge of bankruptcy in the late 1990s? The most sensational collapse to date, the Eaton's story indelibly marked the end of the freewheeling, good-time shopping days of decades past, and the beginning of an era of dramatic changes in the retail environment.

- *The economy has changed.* As we approach the turn of the millennium, the 1990s will be remembered as the lean years – a time when the average Canadian shopper's real after-tax income declined by 7.2% and consumer debt rose from an average of 76% of after-tax income in 1985 to a staggering 114% in 1997. Household savings plummeted to zero in the 1990s, in sharp contrast to the 20% average in the early 1980s. Throughout the 1990s, consumer confidence wavered in response to an unstable dollar, a volatile stock market, and uneasy employment rates. Only the 1930s were worse.

  Today, the retailer's typical customers have less money and are more reluctant to part with their cash or their credit. They wander through an over-stored, competitively heated market, spending their disposable income more wisely and less often. They want comfort, convenience, quality, entertainment, and control – they want it all – and at a good price. They're harder to attract and even harder to hold onto.

- *The marketplace has changed.* Customers may have less after-tax disposable income but they have more options for spending those hard-earned dollars. Retail supply is outstripping demand, a gap that is being intensified with the entry of the Internet's virtual stores. Stretching the walls of the traditional physical store, Web sites bring the mall to the customer's home and offer the ultimate shopping convenience – vast selections and 24-hour-a-day access. As Figure 1.2 illustrates, overall supply, as measured by an index of shopping hours and retail space, has jumped nearly 40%. Yet demand as measured by

**FIGURE 1.2**

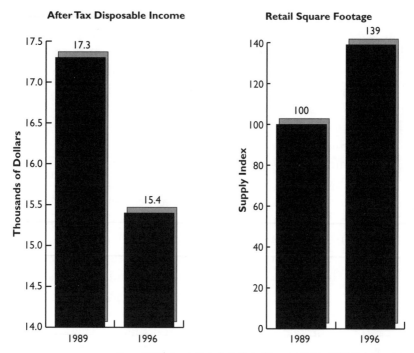

### Supply and Demand in Canadian Retail
Demand has dropped 11% while supply has jumped 40%.

Source: Statistics Canada, Centre for the Study of Commercial Activity (CSCA), Chapters analysis

disposable income has dropped by 11%, driven by the decline in personal disposable income, which was exacerbated by the imposition of GST.

- *Supply has changed.* Retail space is available at a lower cost than the high-rent regional mall that dominated the retail landscape in the 1980s and early 1990s. As illustrated in Figure 1.3, in the Greater Toronto Area (GTA), retail square footage increased more than 50% between 1971 and 1996 – primarily in the big-box format such as Costco's warehouse clubs. Customers may have less to spend but it's certainly easier today to find retailers to take that money.

- *The competition has changed.* Once competing within their own niche or category, retailers now compete with retailers

**FIGURE 1.3**

### Cumulative Growth of New Retail Format
### Floor Space in the GTA 1971-96

New retail format square footage has increased more than 50% since 1971.

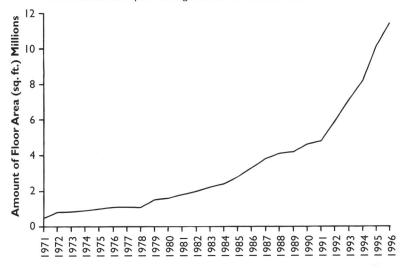

Source: CSCA, 1998

that have extended their categories to offer products and services never before found in that sector. In the grocery sector, it's not enough to keep a competitive watch on Loblaws, IGA, and the others in the same corner of the market. Now there's Costco, Wal-Mart, and others joining in the race for the customer's grocery dollars. And in doing so, they're redefining price, selection, customer service, and convenience in sector after sector.

- *The customer has changed.* Customers are increasingly pressed for time. With few leisure hours, they have less time for shopping, as shown in Figure 1.4. In the last 25 years, the average customer's working hours per week have increased from 41 to 51. Just five years ago, the average Canadian spent 142 hours shopping in a year; now they spend just 40 hours. For the most part, shopping must be quick and purposeful. Retailers respond by extending their shopping hours and selection offerings in their physical stores as well as venturing into Web site storefronts – in an all-out competition for the most precious commodity – the customer's time.

These changing winds and turbulent waters are merciless forces squeezing retailer margins and constraining growth. Retailers are caught trying to increase revenues while coping with shrinking margins and rising costs. Bankruptcies, takeovers, mergers, store openings and closings prevail. Indeed, few industries are characterized by such pronounced cycles of boom and bust as retail.

Yet the power retailers continue to sail at optimum performance levels, consistently outpacing their competitors with an ever-widening gap each leg of the race. Given this tough and hostile environment, what are they doing that enables them to continually win the pennants?

**FIGURE 1.4**

**Work and Leisure Hours**

Today's customers are more time constrained.

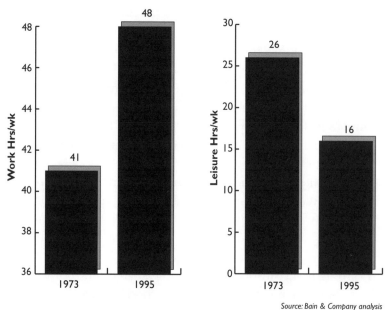

*Source: Bain & Company analysis*

## In Search of the Drivers of Retail Success

Why do the power retailers succeed against the odds? Our study of this retail phenomenon – the polarization of the industry – began with the development of a performance indicator database of North American retailers to analyze the traditional measures that spell success – return on investment (ROI) and return on net assets (RONA). Using annual reports, Value Line (public financial databases), stock performance, and overall growth to create the database, we compared the financial performance of 226 of the largest North American retailers, representing more than $930 billion in sales each year. Each was compared with the others in terms of RONA (we used three-year averages to eliminate the impact of any one-time write-offs or other unique circumstances), sales and sales growth, and stock price performance. For most, this encompassed 1995, 1996, and 1997. For a few, the data included 1994, 1995, and 1996. And for those who had gone bankrupt, the final three years of operation were used. Where possible, we separated the U.S. and Canadian operations of those retailers that span both countries, and isolated the retail side of those companies that also manufacture.

Using the three authors' experiences, and drawing on more than 400 retail assignments performed by Bain & Company worldwide during the 1990s, we then arrayed the retailers on two dimensions:

1. *Relative Market Share (RMS)*: Considering each retailer's chosen market, we determined whether the retailer was dominant (the clear leader, RMS greater than 1.5X), in the thick of it (RMS 0.5–1.4X), or lagging in the market (RMS less than 0.5X), and plotted it on our matrix accordingly. Where possible, we split a national or international retailer's operations into discrete regions, to better assess their true performance.

2. *Retail Value Proposition (RVP) Strength*: Again, for each retailer, we determined its relative RVP strength for its target market. Three levels again were used, the High retailers being those that had a clear advantage in the most important customer segment's most important purchase criteria, the Medium

being those that were neither clearly advantaged nor disadvantaged, or who had an advantage in a criterion or segment that was not critical, and the Low being those that clearly had an offering disadvantage.

---

## BACKGROUND INFORMATION

## THE FIELD RESEARCH – SURVEYS AND INTERVIEWS

Although each author has worked in retailing, or with retailers, for many years, we decided to undertake field research to explore why retail firms had such divergent performance, and in particular, why some firms were clearly power retailers. Prior to developing our own approach, we reviewed recent studies of the Canadian retail industry, such as the *IBM/Retail Council of Canada 1998 CEO Survey* and the *1998 Major Market Retail Report* by Kubas Consultants. We surveyed 70 CEOs and senior executives of Canadian retailers.

Our survey questions asked respondents to describe their firms' strategies and competitive positions, which retail companies they watched most closely for ideas, and which retail principles for success they considered most important.

Our analysis of the survey responses informed our decisions about how to write this book and about what questions to pursue further in a series of personal interviews with retail executives. We then interviewed 20 senior CEOs and presidents from firms representing most sectors of Canadian retailing, for one to two hours each.

One of the most interesting aspects of the interviews was a series of questions on the theme of what "adages for success" they had learned over the years. We have benefited from the principles and the wisdom offered to us in these interviews. Our analysis, the senior executive survey, and the interviews formed the foundation for this book.

---

Market share leadership and a clear RVP were characteristics shared by the power retailers. From this perspective, we grouped the retailers in our study into three distinct categories based on each retailer's RVP and market share position:

- *Power Retailers* – retailers whose performance reflects a high RVP and high market share, truly those that have ability, strength, and authority.
- *The Pack* – retailers who are in the middle of the pack on both RVP and market share. They may excel on one of the dimensions, but not both.
- *The Precarious* – retailers who were low on both RVP and market share and whose futures are uncertain, unstable, or insecure.

The relative position of these retailers is illustrated in Figure 1.5 below – the horizontal depicts strength or leadership in market share; the vertical, the retail value proposition. These two dimensions, RVP and RMS, drive wide variations in financial performance. As shown in Figure 1.6, power retailers earned RONA of 15.4%, clearly outperforming the pack, which achieved 8.6%, and the precarious, who only broke even.

**FIGURE 1.5**

**Positioning**

Three distinct groups of retailers emerged from our study, based on performance on two dimensions.

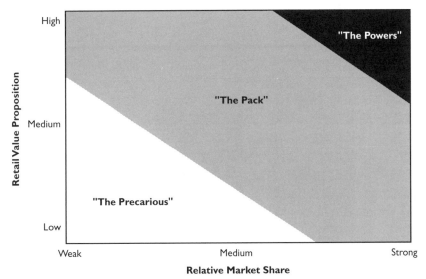

Source: Dow Jones, Bain & Company analysis

What accounted for the superior financial performance of the power retailers? The power retailers followed four principles of retailing:

1. Deliver a customer-driven superior Retail Value Proposition (RVP).
2. Achieve the leadership position in geographic markets, categories, and channels.
3. Execute better than competitors in the areas of people, technology, and costs.
4. Lead change by continually reinventing the organization.

## The First Principle of Retail Success

### ▪ *Deliver a Customer-driven, Superior Retail Value Proposition (RVP)*

The power retailers consistently win the race because they

**FIGURE 1.6**

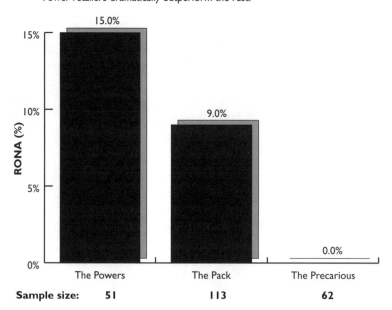

## Return on Net Assets (RONA) by Category
Power retailers dramatically outperform the rest.

| | | |
|---|---|---|
| The Powers | The Pack | The Precarious |
| 15.0% | 9.0% | 0.0% |

RONA (%)

Sample size: 51     113     62

*Source: Canada Disclosure; Standards & Poor Stock Prices;*
*Hoover's Online; OneSource; Annual Reports*

focus all of their attention on being the best in their niche or category. They establish a clear position in their customers' minds and then deliver on their promise.

Figure 1.7 illustrates how the retailers in our study who had superior RVP outperformed the competition.

RVP encompasses four key dimensions:

1. selection
2. customer experience
3. price, and
4. convenience

**FIGURE 1.7**
## RONA by RVP
RVP-superior retailers earned 15% RONA,
compared to RVP-weak retailers that lost money.

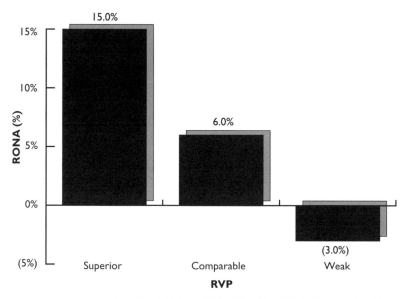

Source: Canada Disclosure; S&P Stock Prices; Hoover's Online; OneSource; Annual Reports

While each of these dimensions is important in various ways for any retailer's success, the power retailers balance and focus them to deliver foremost what their customers value.

RVP is the brand proposition, the promise that the retailer represents to customers:

- Home Depot and Toys "R" Us represent selection.
- Nordstrom, Holt Renfrew, and Harry Rosen represent customer experience.
- Price Club/Costco, Wal-Mart, and Winners represent price.
- CDNow and Becker's represent convenience.

*Power retailers focus their entire team and business strategies on one key dimension of the customer-driven RVP. The successful RVP only evolves when management knows its target customer, its own competitive advantage, and is poised to fulfill the promise it makes through superior execution.*

Customer-driven, the RVP is the retailer's means for establishing and sustaining a gap between itself and its competitors.

In formulating their RVP strategy, the power retailers research and segment the potential customer base, identify the most profitable customers, and then focus all of their efforts on delivering the value that they know will attract and sustain that customer. While there's a myriad of factors that can attract customers, the winners focus their entire team and business strategies on one key dimension of the customer-driven RVP – be it a broader selection of products, added convenience, superior or more personalized service, or the lowest price in town.

But the RVP doesn't just happen. It's a process that the management team must lead. The successful RVP can only evolve when the management team can clearly:
- define the target customer
- determine its own competitive advantage, and
- deliver the promise through superior execution.

### The Second Principle of Retail Success

## Achieve the Leadership Position in Geographic Markets, Categories, and Channels

The next stage of our research centred on examining another similarity in power retailers' profiles: they hold the number-one position in market share in their sector. How do the winners

## WALGREEN'S – COMPETING THROUGH CONVENIENCE

**AN INSIDE LOOK**

The U.S. pharmacy chain, Walgreen's, is a master in achieving a leadership position in the market with its RVP focus on convenience. During the period 1986 to 1996, its stock appreciated an outstanding 270%. Today, the $15 billion operation has 2,549 stores, averaging 14,000 square feet and 18,000 SKUs of merchandise.

The key to Walgreen's success? The entire organization is focused on delivering three key dimensions of convenience to its customers: a handy location, fast and efficient transactions, and a customer prescription database that can be accessed at any one of its stores across the nation.

The Walgreen's customer values convenience over all else and Walgreen's delivers. It locates each store at "Main & Main" in the communities it serves, with plenty of free parking. Checkouts are equipped with scanners to ensure fast and efficient transactions and few line-ups. Over 1,100 of its stores have drive-through windows so customers can pick up prescriptions with a minimum expenditure of time and energy. Over 500 locations operate 24 hours a day. Its satellite-based computer system, Intercon, maintains a central database of all of its customers' prescription records, so they can be accessed from any store. Customers who forget to pack a prescription for a trip know that a replacement can be easily picked up at the Walgreen's at their destination. While the pharmacy is the major draw at a Walgreen's store, customers also value the convenience of departments such as cosmetics, greeting cards, non-prescription drugs, and photo-finishing.

For 22 consecutive years, Walgreen's has achieved record sales and earnings. And this power retailer's strategy doesn't stop there. Walgreen's has announced plans to expand to 3,000 stores by the year 2000 and to 6,000 by 2010.

achieve the winning position? Moreover, how do they sustain it? Retail winners focus on leading in their target geographic markets, in their product categories, and in the channels – that is, the retail venues they use, whether bricks-and-mortar or virtual. The CEOs of the power retailers share our perspective that market share drives financial performance. Consequently, they choose their markets carefully and enter them knowing they can achieve the number-one position. In 1987, Builders Square, a Home Depot competitor, opened four stores in the Atlanta market. This was a direct assault on Home Depot's home turf in a market where Home Depot had both its headquarters and 13 stores. Home Depot's market dominance in Atlanta led to Builders Square closing its Atlanta stores in 1991. If power retailers slip to a second or third position in a local market, they either realign their strategies to overtake the number-one competitor or exit that market. They don't choose to languish as a distant follower. Our study clearly highlighted that market-share leaders outperformed the competition. As Figure 1.8 illustrates, market leaders earned dramatically more than other retailers. In fact, the failure of many Canadian retailers in the U.S. can be attributed to violating this second principle. Recent withdrawals from the American market by Future Shop and Second Cup illustrate this point.

**FIGURE 1.8**

### RONA by RMS

Leaders earned 12% RONA, compared to followers that earned up to 8%.

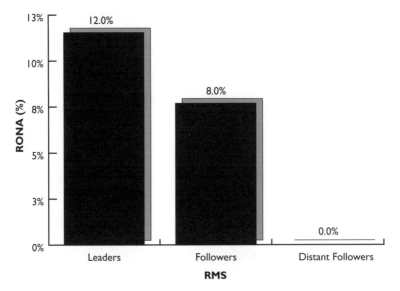

*Source: Canada Disclosure; S&P Stock Prices; Hoover's Online; OneSource; Annual Reports*

## AN INSIDE LOOK

## FUTURE SHOP – NUMBER ONE IN ELECTRONICS IN CANADA

In the electronics landscape of the mid-90s, Future Shop was both a power retailer and a follower. In Canada, it dominates its market; in the U.S. it was slipping into a precarious abyss of losses.

By year-end March 1998, the Canadian operation made $31.2 million on sales of $1.25 billion. This strong number-one position in Canada brings significant competitive advantage in both buying and in customer share of mind. In sharp contrast, the U.S. operation lost $27.3 million on sales of $509 million in the same fiscal period. Overall, Future Shop in the U.S. lost more than $50 million over two years as it tried to compete with larger U.S. retailers such as Circuit City and Best Buy. As one analyst pointed out, "They don't have the purchasing power of the U.S. rivals."

**Future Shop return on sales (year ending March 31, 1998)**

Clearly, market share heavily influenced Future Shop's profit performance. Future Shop could not succeed in the U.S., just as Computer City could not make it in Canada because of its follower status north of the border. Future Shop, recognizing the importance of market leadership, announced in early 1999 that it was exiting the U.S. market to concentrate on the Canadian market. The stock market applauded the move, driving its stock price up 25% after the announcement. In November 1998, Computer City sold its seven Canadian stores to Future Shop.

## The Third Principle of Retail Success

■ *Execute Better than Competitors in the Areas of People, Technology, and Costs.*

We next examined the power retailers' execution in the areas of people, costs, and technology. As shown in Figure 1.9, the average power retailer earned a 15% return on net assets, but the variation around this average was so large that it clearly demonstrated that RVP and market share are not the only drivers of financial performance.

**FIGURE 1.9**

**RONA Ranges**

RVP and RMS explain only part of a retail success.

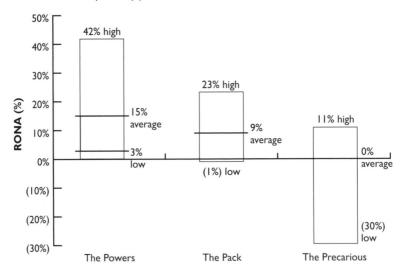

Source: RONA Database

The strongest power retailers earned returns above 40% while the weakest performers in the group barely earned 3% RONA. Since these retailers all followed principles one and two, the variation had to be attributed to other factors. The difference was execution in the areas of people, costs, and technology. Clearly the strongest power retailers excel in all of these critical factors. They invest in their people, they control costs, and they manage technology far better than their competitors.

A superior RVP leads to a gain in market share and eventual market leadership. RVP combined with market leadership gives the profit and the potential to excel in execution. And a superior execution leads to a continuous improvement in RVP, creating a virtuous circle for retailers, as shown in Figure 1.10.

**FIGURE 1.10**

## Virtuous Circle for Retail Success

## HOME DEPOT – A COMMITMENT TO ITS PEOPLE

Since it first opened its doors in 1978, Home Depot has rapidly become the largest home improvement company in North America, most recently achieving nine consecutive years of record earnings and profits. The cornerstone of its success? Home Depot cares about its people.

The Home Depot credo, drafted by its own employees and given to all new staff, communicates a corporate culture that inspires, respects, and involves everyone who works within it:

**The Home Depot culture is about people – caring human beings who**
- value our customers
- respect fellow associates
- treat our vendors as partners
- love what they do
- feel good about themselves
- are allowed to make mistakes, learn from them and move on
- are creative and have an entrepreneurial spirit
- know they can make a difference
- ask questions and suggest new ways
- welcome change

Annette Verschuren, President of Home Depot Canada, proudly states, "Excellent people equals excellent service. It is not a cost, it's an investment." Employees with pressing family problems can take up to six months' leave. The company offers an adoption assistance program. When employees donate to charities, it matches their donations dollar for dollar. During the Hurricane Andrew crisis in Florida, while other vendors profited from the disaster, Home Depot issued a no-profit policy and sold much of its lumber at a loss.

To encourage its employees' commitment to the organization, Home Depot helps them become owners. All full-time employees receive 7% of their salary in stock and can purchase stock twice a year at a discount. Assistant store managers and higher positions receive even higher stock options. With its headquarters aptly called the "Home Depot Support

Centre," Home Depot has decentralized its management and decision-making while encouraging all employees to think like the owners they are. These incentives are so successful that an impressive 95% of its employees voluntarily participate in its quarterly "breakfast" store meetings, delivered live via satellite at 6:30 on a Sunday morning and designed to encourage candid feedback.

Home Depot encourages employees to be the very best they can and delivers the extensive training that will help them achieve their goals. As Home Depot's co-founder Bernie Marcus explains, "People looking for just a job –we don't want those kind of people here. People looking for a career – these are the kind of people we want."

Employees who bought $1,000 worth of stock in 1982 now have shares that are worth more than $150,000. As David Glass, CEO of Wal-Mart, says, "I think Home Depot is the best managed company in America, ours included" – high praise from a retail champ. According to Arthur Blank, co-founder and current CEO, "Taking care of customers is incredibly important – but the way you take care of customers in our business is by taking care of the people who take care of the customers." Home Depot knows that when it treats its people well, each and every employee will treat its customers well. Its commitment to its people has made Home Depot the $30 billion business it is today and has led to its twice being ranked as the most admired retailer in the U.S. by *Fortune*.

## The Fourth Principle of Retail Success

### ▦ *Lead Change by Continually Reinventing the Organization*

Picture the opposite scenario of the virtuous circle we have just described: those retailers who don't follow, or follow only some of, the first three principles, soon find themselves on a doom loop. These are the retailers who spiral downward in varying degrees, some to the point of restructuring and others to the point of bankruptcy. The first three principles act as the compass for plotting the organization's direction and help it reach its destination of greater success. But any strategy will eventually fail. Power retailers know that historical success is no guarantee

FIGURE 1.11
## Virtuous Circle for Retail Success

of future success or even of survival; change is a certainty. So they embrace change, they know when to chart a new course for the organization, when to bring new players onboard, and how to stay focused all the while – and that sometimes they must reinvent themselves to affect any other worthwhile change.

The virtuous circle has the potential of becoming a doom loop if the retailer does not adapt all three first principles in the face of change in the retail environment. (See Figure 1.11.)

## LOBLAW – LEADING CHANGE

**AN INSIDE LOOK**

Loblaw's success in the 1990s is so dramatic it's easy to forget the company's weak position just 15 years earlier. In 1976, Loblaw was losing $50 million on annual sales of $3.5 billion. That same year, Richard Currie took the helm as President of Loblaw to lead the changes that would make the organization a phenomenal success.

As Currie said in a Harvard Business School case on Loblaw, "I found a situation where we were hemorrhaging red ink, losing

$50 million a year; we had no cash; I was at the controls of a huge unwieldy beast of a corporation and the true question I faced was, here we are headed straight downhill, how do we stop the train?"

Currie did more than stop the train; he changed its direction. Within one year, he turned the loss that he had inherited. By 1984, the company had almost doubled sales and was earning profits of $64 million and was well on its way to its number-one position in the grocery sector today.

Currie led change. He and his team focused on stopping the losses and raising the cash needed to develop new retail formats and to invest aggressively in remodelling its stores. They centralized finance, real estate, and procurement to gain control over key operating decisions. By centralizing procurement years before its Canadian competitors, Loblaw improved margins to the highest level in the industry.

A March 1976 study had found that only 3% of Loblaw's Ontario customers perceived it to be price-competitive. Currie invested in information technology and repositioned the company in consumers' minds. He lowered prices, improved selection, introduced innovative private label products – the No Name value products and the President's Choice prestige line – and dramatically changed the organization's market position.

The results under Currie's leadership are a textbook classic of the power of managing change. On all financial metrics, Loblaw led the Canadian food retail industry in the 1990s. In 1998, it earned $370 million on sales of $12 billion. It trades at a price/earning ratio (P/E) multiple that is double that of its Canadian competitors – a position that gives it tremendous currency to add to its market leadership position. It has 36% share of the Canadian grocery industry, and with its acquisition of Provigo, has established itself as a strong number-one or co-number-one in every regional market except the West. Loblaw continues to innovate with new and exciting stores and new products like President's Choice banking. Deservedly, Currie was chosen as the 1997 Retailer of the Year by the Retail Council of Canada.

# "Great Books are Just the Beginning"

The Chapters' tag line aptly reflects its customers' experience as they enter any one of the 64 superstores or 250 traditional stores. The superstores are simply Chapters; the traditional stores operate under the names Coles, SmithBooks, LibrairieSmith, Classic Books, and The Book Company. Together they represent the fastest expansion in specialty retail this past decade and Canada's largest book retailer.

## Underpinning Chapters' Success: The Four Principles for Retail Success

In the past four years, Chapters' performance has been outstanding with its retail net income rising by a factor of 20 and its revenues tripling. Total revenues in fiscal 1999 grew by 25% to $572 million compared to $457 million during the previous fiscal year. Revenues from superstores for fiscal 1999 were $297 million, compared to $167 million in 1998. As Chief Financial Officer Tamara Lawson notes, "We quadrupled our superstore revenues in the last two years, and have now built a business which accounts for more than half of Chapters' revenues – all this from a standing start in 1995."

The strategy for this banner performance? The four principles presented throughout this book. Following these principles, Chapters has achieved not only extraordinary success but has revolutionized the way books are sold.

## The Chapters' Story

The Chapters' story began in 1995 with the merger of SmithBooks and Coles Bookstores. Pathfinder Capital had acquired SmithBooks in May of 1994 with a plan to buy Coles and merge these two leading Canadian bookstores. The strategy was to build a strong base company through the existing traditional mall stores, and using the cash generated from these operations, expand into its new vision of operations: the large-format book superstore.

Less than six months after the April 1995 merger, Chapters launched its first superstore in Burlington, Ontario. A week later, it opened its second Chapters in Burnaby, British Columbia. Both stores won rave reviews from their customers and were immediate financial successes.

Confident of the public's acceptance of this new concept in book buying, Chapters opened seven more superstores the following year and 18 more in progressive stages soon after. As Dan Soper, Senior Vice-President of Large-Format Operations, notes, "Chapters added more square footage to the retail book sector in just one year [1998] than Coles Bookstores had built in its forty years of operations."

## Number of Chapters Superstores

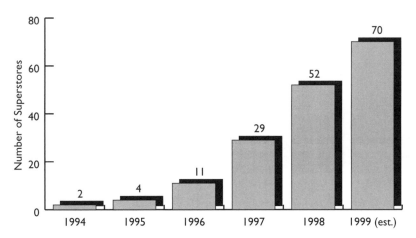

The retail value proposition Chapters represents is a huge *selection* of books, magazines, CD-ROMs, and music. *Convenience* is offered through the accessible locations, extended hours, and knowledgeable staff. An appealing *buyer experience* is delivered through numerous events such as book readings and music performances, as well as through the decor and the refreshments of the onsite Starbucks café, which encourages customers to browse the merchandise comfortably in couches or armchairs with a cup of coffee and biscotti at their elbow. Finally, Chapters builds customer loyalty with programs of discounts, rewards, special offers and invitations.

While the cash registers tally the overwhelming response of its customers, the retail industry itself has presented Chapters with numerous awards since its inception in 1995. In 1998, for the second consecutive year (and confirmed for 1999 as well), the prestigious Kubas Customer

Survey rated Chapters as the best all-around retailer on a composite score among 130 retailers. The customer rating includes performance on selection, customer service, store layout and decor, and value for dollars spent.

## Chapters Rated #1 of 130 Retailers on Overall Composite Score

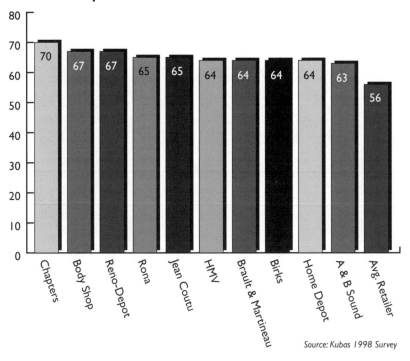

Source: Kubas 1998 Survey

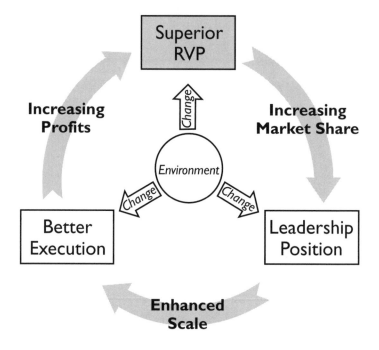

---

## PRINCIPLE 1:

## Deliver a Customer-driven Superior, Retail Value Proposition

**Chapter 2:** THE BASIS FOR STRATEGY–CUSTOMER SEGMENTATION

**1.** Needs-based segmentation is the critical first step in designing a differentiated RVP.

**2.** More attractive segments include those which buy high-margin products, are growing, have a lower cost to serve, are loyal, and are predisposed to a retailer's existing RVP.

**3.** Power retailers make the difficult tradeoffs required to dominate their target segments.

**Chapter 3:** THE ESSENCE OF RETAIL DIFFERENTIATION – THE RETAIL VALUE PROPOSITION

**1.** The retail value proposition is the promise made to customers about what they can expect from the retailer. This promise is the essence of the brand.

**2.** The RVP is the benefits including selection, customer experience, and convenience that a retailer delivers in exchange for the price paid.

**3.** Power retailers choose one of the four elements of RVP on which to excel as the core of their differentiation strategy, while still offering acceptable levels of performance in the remaining three.

# 2 The Basis for Strategy – Customer Segmentation

*"Focus is the key. You need to segment the market. You can't be all things to all people. And once you choose your course, you can't veer off from it; even if you can do some things that are attractive on their own, you can't do them if they don't fit your target segment."*

– David Bloom, Chief Executive Officer,
Shoppers Drug Mart

Is there a retailer around that doesn't brag about "customer knowledge" to anyone who will listen? But what separates the power retailers from the pack is the depth and usefulness of this so-called knowledge. It's the difference between knowing the demographics of your customers and knowing precisely what need is being fulfilled. Unfortunately, while everyone talks of customer segmentation as the basis for strategy, only a few are able to truly benefit from its potential.

In this chapter, we will describe the manner in which the power retailers apply customer segmentation. They go well beyond the catch-all generic segments to get down to specific, identifiable groups, whom they can serve better than any of their competitors. Rather than identifying their target customers simply as, say, females with household incomes greater than $45,000, they know that their target customers are convenience-oriented, largely price-insensitive, and service-focused, who want full shelves, empty checkout lines, and prices within 12% of the lowest-price competition. With this information, a retailer now can make some critical decisions.

Although the concept is simple, the process and methodology of segmentation are quite complex. They may actually be daunting enough to deter many retailers faced with a segmentation effort. The reality is that far too many retailers segment in only a superficial manner. If segmentation is done at the "30,000-foot level" ("I can see people down there, but I can't determine anything new about them") then it's useless. The power retailers get ahead of the pack by making the segmentation so specific that it becomes controversial even within their own organizations. The acid test of segmentation usefulness occurs when specific, hard choices are faced, choices which have major implications for strategy.

## Segment for Profit, Not Revenue

Lakeside Clothiers (disguised name), an apparel and accessories retailer, was grappling with how to solidify and improve performance across markets. Although it was quite profitable, Lakeside suffered from uneven performance, and did not perform at anything approaching its full potential. It was facing increased competition from traditional and new sources, and had not developed a coherent response to protect its business.

*Power retailers get ahead of the pack by making segmentation so specific that it becomes controversial even within their own organizations.*

A segmentation study identified the 22% of customers who provided 76% of the profit, and detailed which specific group of customers the retailer had to focus on to be successful, as shown in Figure 2.1. This target segment, women who valued selection (breadth was more valuable than depth), was called "selection-focused" by Lakeside. "Selection-focused" women demanded the widest possible variety and were willing to forego both price and convenience to receive this selection. This forced Lakeside management to make difficult decisions regarding store size, pricing strategy and store locations. Based on a detailed examination of this segment, $33 million in incremental contribution from the stores was achieved through tailoring the offering to this segment, by increasing selection in some categories while cutting out others, by reallocating advertising expense to specific channels, and by introducing "preferred customer" services to this group of clients. Though revenue was nearly flat, this $33 million contribution increase was 50% above the historic level of contribution from the stores.

The Lakeside example is instructive in that the management did not define its target in a nebulous way, it was very specific: "This segment generates our profit, so we had better serve them better than anyone else can, because if we lose one of them and replace them with one from another segment, we lose money." This implied that Lakeside looked at profits, not revenue, for guidance, and that a dollar of revenue from some customers is worth far more than a dollar from others. Simply stated, the customer that is loyal and buys higher-margin products is worth more than any other customer.

"Top line is a retail aphrodisiac," says Elliott Wahle, President and CEO of Dylex, who explains that his company is completely hooked on profits. "Anyone can grow, but we are interested only in profitable growth." This sentiment sums up what the power retailers base their strategies on: That all dollars of revenue are not equal; that revenue is not the goal, since it all comes down to profits in the end.

Developing a winning, sustainable retail value proposition (we will discuss RVP in the next chapter) is the foundation on which retail strategy is built. And this competition for the hearts, minds, and wallets of customers can only be won by first using the tool of customer segmentation. Customer segmentation allows the retailer to identify attractive target-customer groups that it intends to serve better than any other retailer.

Power retailers have long since realized that there are inherent and complex tradeoffs that must be made in order to benefit

**FIGURE 2.1**

### Lakeside Clothiers: Segmentation

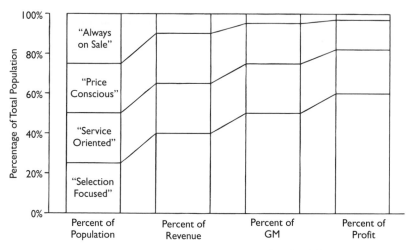

Source: Bain & Company segmentation study

from segmentation. The days of being all things to all people, if this was ever possible, are certainly over, as the segments in nearly every retail category are just too well developed. In sporting goods, for example, certain segments want the absolute lowest prices, and are willing to be inconvenienced to save money, while other customers value high service and convenience. Clearly, the sporting goods retailer cannot attract both of these segments, as lowest prices demand lowest costs (remember, it's profit, not revenue, that counts) and high convenience (more stores, more expensive rent) and high service (more expensive labour) entail higher costs. So the retailer must make a choice: "Do I focus on the high-convenience or the low-price segment?" Taking the middle road – trying to please both – is a recipe for disaster, as the retailer would end up being the second or even third choice for each segment. It's critical to be the first choice for one segment, at a minimum.

Peter Luckhurst, the President of HMV Canada, sums this concept up: "In terms of strategy, we are a specialty retailer. Twenty percent of the population buys 80% of the music and it is this 20% that we cater to. We are definitely not for everybody – if you are nuts about music, as we ourselves are, then we are for you. If you're not, then we're not. We compete on quality and service, not on price alone. While we want to be fair in our pricing, we cannot be the lowest price, or we would be competing with Wal-Mart, which would mean driving costs out of our business. Lowest-cost would force us to do things that would be completely counter to what our core customer needs."

## Needs-Driven Segmentation

The harsh reality is that coming up with actionable, accurate, and proprietary segmentation requires a great deal of data that is rarely straightforward to obtain. While many options for segmentation exist, the power retailers rely on needs-based segmentation to provide the real insights that lead to concrete actions and competitive advantage. The reality is that demographics such as age, income, and home ownership are nice to know but don't help in improving the retail value proposition. Behavioural segmentation, such as who drinks coffee and who does not, adds some details about purchasing patterns, but doesn't get at the root cause for the purchase – that is, the *need* that the purchasing behaviour is satisfying.

*The days of being all things to all people are over. Customer segmentation allows the retailer to identify attractive target-customer groups that it intends to serve better than any other retailer.*

Needs-based segmentation is complex. For this reason, we have chosen one power retailer to illustrate this approach from start to finish. We will outline one example of a power retailer in some detail, in order to describe segmentation in some detail.

With more than 800 stores, Shoppers Drug Mart has positioned itself as Canada's leading drug store chain for almost 30 years. Initially, the company's coast-to-coast stores were very successful at both the pharmacy side of the business as well as in general merchandise. However, by the mid-1990s, with competitors beginning to breathe down their necks and a flattening of profits, it was clear that the company needed to rethink its core strategy.

Like many other retailers, Shoppers had tried to be everything to all people (its former slogan was: "Everything you want in a drug store"). And like retailers who built their strategy around this concept, Shoppers was in danger of becoming second-choice for all customers. The competitive scene had become much more difficult during the late '80s and early '90s, and to its credit, Shoppers' executives were willing to rethink the strategy before performance deteriorated. New entrants, such as Wal-Mart, began encroaching on Shoppers' front-store profitability. To add to its woes, national supermarket chains began opening in-store pharmacies in addition to health and beauty sections.

David Bloom, Shoppers' CEO and the Retail Council of Canada's Retailer of the Year in 1996, says, "Food/drug combos and mass merchandisers are two very large competitors. But we have to play the game on our own playing field, and this means having some self-control. If we play on the value-added playing field, offering multiple consumer benefits to our most valuable customers, fully satisfying this customer, we'll be in great shape."

## Performing the Segmentation

Shoppers Drug Mart's experience is a textbook example of how to perform customer segmentation. In addition to the qualitative research which began the effort – more than 20 focus groups were held – more than 3,000 quantitative interviews were also conducted. While the focus groups helped to develop and confirm hypotheses regarding what drives customer attitudes and segmentation, the interviews served to quantify the size and value of the segments.

Bain & Company conducted these interviews by telephone, sampling in the trade radius of 40 stores nationwide, with 75 respondents per store. Stores were selected to represent all types of stores (region, trend sales, profit trend, location type, competitor set and strength, and other factors). The data were then analyzed in many different ways to determine the segments that existed, and the attractiveness of each.

## CUSTOMER INTERVIEWS – THE ART AND THE SCIENCE

Knowing what to ask in segmentation interviews is at least as much art as it is science. For example, in fashion retailing, some key question areas would include:

**Attitudes towards store selection criteria**
- price sensitivity
- selection breadth (categories carried)
- selection depth (number of choices within a category)
- style focus (fashion forward vs. classic conservative, etc.)
- quality requirements
- brand-name focus
- service components (e.g., speed of checkout, salesperson, advice, etc.)
- convenience of location

**Apparel shopping behaviour**
- familiarity with specific stores
- past year shopping profile
  - stores visited/frequency
  - stores where made purchase/frequency
  - dollars spent at each store
  - spending vs. one year ago (more, less, or the same)
  - reasons for spending change vs. one year ago
  - future intentions

**Store evaluation criteria**
- price
  - overall prices
  - sales/promotions
- selection
  - breadth
  - depth
- apparel style
  - fashion forward vs. classic conservative
  - carries styles looking for

- apparel quality/brand focus
- service
  - speed of checkout
  - helpful, knowledgeable salespeople
  - salespeople available to give advice
  - free alterations
  - return policy
- in-store operations
  - in-stock position (always has size/colour in stock)
  - ease of finding what looking for
  - hours
  - store credit card

### Demographics
- age, sex, income, household size, marital status, education, etc.

The next step involved detailed, quantitative research focused on measuring the size and the value of the different segments, their current shopping behaviour, and their current perceptions of both Shoppers and its key competitors. Bain carried out another telephone survey, again sampling around a radius of 40 Shoppers stores representing all five of its regions coast-to-coast.

Completing several analyses of those customers, Bain and Shoppers determined five distinct customer segments, as shown in Figures 2.2 and 2.3:

- price-insensitive convenience shoppers
- self-serve make-it-easy shoppers
- health-focused advice-seeker shoppers
- price-conscious shoppers
- price-focused "cherry pickers" (those shoppers who will travel from store to store in order to obtain the best price on every item)

**FIGURE 2.2**

**Spending/Profitability Profile**
Target segments account for 45% of revenue, 59% of total direct profit and 71% of front shop direct profit.

*\*Disguised Data*
*Source: Consumer Research; PLP Model*

The latter two groups were largely going to Wal-Mart. With its 800 locations very much oriented around convenience, Shoppers determined it could not attract these shoppers in any sort of profitable way. The first three segments represented the bulk of Shoppers' profits, and to compete with Wal-Mart on price was a game it could not win without alienating these top three categories of customers.

Shoppers determined the most profitable strategy was to focus on three of the five identified segments:

- the price-insensitive convenience shoppers
- the self-serve make-it-easy shoppers
- the health-focused advice-seekers

## FIGURE 2.3

**Market Share by Segment**

Shoppers Drug Mart captures a greater share of the three target segments' spending.

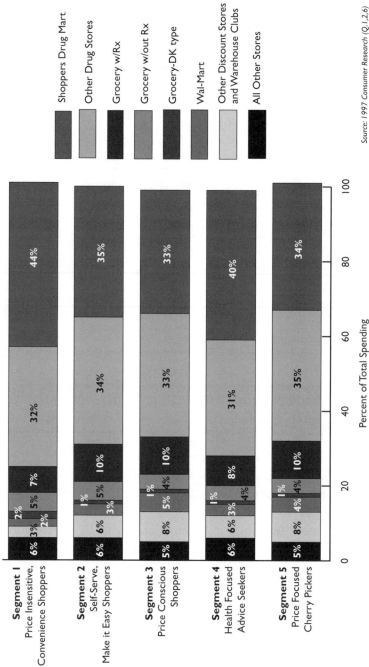

Source: 1997 Consumer Research (Q.1,2,6)

## ■ *Price-Insensitive Convenience Shoppers*

Price-insensitive shoppers were those consumers who chose stores that were "easy to shop" and easy to "get in and out of quickly" and were "located close by." They were not at all price-sensitive and were definitely willing to pay more for these "ease of shopping" features. Having said this, they also did not want to be taken advantage of in retail pricing – prices had to be within an acceptable range. They also had relatively high service needs, including basic service (e.g., knowledgeable sales staff) and "advice-type" service. These consumers accounted for 12%* of the total drug store customer population; Shoppers received a 50%* share of their total spending on drug store products.

## ■ *Self-Serve Make-It-Easy Shoppers*

These consumers were also focused on stores that were "easy to shop," easy to "get in and out of quickly," and "located close by." They were not price-sensitive and were also willing to pay more for these features. However, the low service needs of this group clearly differentiated it from the first group above. While these consumers didn't mind service being available in the store, they were unlikely to ask for help or advice. In all, they made up 30%* of the total population of the target customers. Shoppers received 40%* of their total spending on drug store purchases.

## ■ *Health-Focused Advice-Seekers*

Like the two groups above, these consumers also chose the easy-to-shop stores; however, they demonstrated the highest focus on service. They wanted knowledgeable sales staff that provided both basic service and "advice-type" service for pharmaceuticals, over-the-counter aids, and cosmetics. They also stated clearly their need for adequate selection (e.g., breadth and depth) and perceived Shoppers as satisfying that need.

Using this segment information, Shoppers was able to orient its stores to meet the needs of these customers. They took items

---

*\*Data have been disguised.*

out of the aisles in order to make their stores even more convenient, chose many more convenient locations as opposed to "destination superstores," and completely refocused the business around these key segments.

BACKGROUND INFORMATION

## THE ESSENCE OF SUPERIOR CUSTOMER SEGMENTATION

As an indicator of quality, segmentation data must measure up to standard on five key dimensions. It must be:

- meaningful
- Mutually Exclusive and Collectively Exhaustive (MECE)
- measurable
- substantial, and
- actionable.

### 1. Meaningful

Segmentation must be meaningful; that is, there should be enough differentiation among segments such that each segment appears unique. Segmentation that allows all potential customers to be part of every potential segment is not useful to the retailer. The retailer needs to be able to determine that one group of customers exhibits different traits from another group. It is clear in the Shoppers example that the price-sensitive "cherry pickers" require a completely different retail value proposition from the convenience-oriented segment.

### 2. MECE

Each segment should represent a target group that is Mutually Exclusive and Collectively Exhaustive (MECE). By carefully focusing on a segment, the retailer can ensure each customer group belongs to one, and only one, segment; there should be no overlaps with customers placed in more than one group. No customer in the Shoppers case belongs to two segments, as they are very different from one another. No one, for example, could be members of both the convenience and the advice-seeking segments – if they had, then it would indicate that perhaps these two segments are actually only one, or that there existed a third meaningful segment.

## 3. Measurable

Each segment should be measurable; that is, it should be clearly defined with a market share that can be quantified. In other words, the retailer needs to be able to determine its market share of each particular group of customer segments. This allows Shoppers, for example, to readily determine where it is winning, where competitors are doing better by focusing on a specific set of segments, and where to focus its efforts on developing an RVP that beats the competitors. If they already have the dominant share of the convenience segment, surely it makes sense to begin the quest for increased profits here, as opposed to throwing out its current advantages and beginning with another segment where Shoppers is a distant player.

## 4. Substantial

Each segment should be substantial; that is, there should be sufficient numbers in each segment to merit analysis and targeting. Those segments that have very low populations generally are not considered to be relevant, as they are too small to warrant investment. This is where the quantity of the data is critical – a retailer has to be confident that these segments actually exist. In the Shoppers example, the five segments made intuitive sense (always a good acid test), but it took more than 3,000 open-ended and lengthy interviews to prove that they actually existed, in what relative proportions, and with enough detail to draw meaningful conclusions.

## 5. Actionable

The segment should be actionable – that is, the retailer can design an RVP that will attract and sustain that segment. Telling a retailer to focus on the segment that has blue eyes isn't going to get them very far. The segments identified must be relevant to the retailer in order to guide media choices, channel decisions, and so on.

Collecting and crunching the data to identify customer segments is obviously necessary but alone this process is insufficient to grow profitability. To begin developing a winning retail value proposition to attract the most profitable segments, the retailer must first prioritize the segments.

## Choosing a Target Segment

What makes a target group attractive? Attractiveness of a segment is comprised of three different elements:

- The revenue potential, which essentially refers to the size of the segment, its growth potential, what it buys, how much and how often.
- The cost to serve the segment, including considerations such as buyer power, product requirements, price sensitivity, advertising requirements, channel and service requirements.
- The capacity of the segment to become loyal customers. The term "lifetime value" is used to assess each segment's loyalty and value over a multi-year period, not just its profitability in this given period.

Revenue potential is obvious, but many retailers fail to calculate the cost of serving certain customer segments. For example, banks may underestimate the cost of serving older clients, who prefer to deal with tellers rather than use the ATMs.

*Power retailers look at profits, not revenue, for guidance when considering the market segment to cater to, and recognize that a dollar from some customers is worth far more than a dollar from others.*

The capacity for loyalty is similarly a very important and often overlooked factor in selecting those groups that are most profitable. Obviously, customers that are more loyal over time are worth more to the retailer. Those that come into a retailer's store once because of some particularly bold advertising then never revisit often represent customers from whom the retailer actually loses money. It is only through repeat visits that the

## OFFICE SUPPLIES SUPPLIERS – TARGETING DIFFERENT SEGMENTS

**AN INSIDE LOOK**

Other lessons in the power of segmentation come from the office supplies market, in which both Grand & Toy and Business Depot compete. But they focus on very different segments of the market, with Grand & Toy concentrating on large corporate clients while Business Depot's core segment is home or small offices.

Ed Harsant, Business Depot's CEO, says "The key is to stay very focused. We say we have 'everything you need for your office' and that means everything that fits under that umbrella, for the small or home office. These small offices want low prices and one-stop shopping, so we ensure that we deliver on these two dimensions. And we rethink our product mix in line with this – we are getting into copy centres now." He makes the point that Business Depot concerns itself with only "the consumable side of what our customers need. We don't want to sell computers or copiers or cell phones – we can't compete at the service element for these products."

Grand & Toy has a different approach, as it goes after the commercial, or contract, segment. "The commercial client cares about us being in-stock and offering fast delivery, all at a volume-discounted price," says Peter Vanexan, Grand & Toy's President. "We carry a better line of merchandise in our stores than you'd get for your home office because our stores are there for the commercial customer to shop at when they are in a hurry. We're a commercial business that has a retail channel, rather than a retailer with a commercial arm." He adds, "We are quite good at tracking our customers. We're really into database marketing, and we can send personalized flyers that say, 'This month we have paper on sale that matches the fax machine you bought,' and it really works."

"share of wallet" (the percentage of the individual's shopping) will improve. Loyal customers shop at a particular store more frequently and tend to stay for longer periods of time than those who just go wherever the latest pricing initiative leads them. Thus loyalty plays a very important part of how a retailer might assess target segments as well.

The matrix in Figure 2.4 prioritizes segments based on the attractiveness of each and the retailer's ability to serve in a differentiated way. Obviously, if a segment is both attractive and can be served in a differentiated way, it should be a priority. If the retailer has little capability to serve this group in a differentiated way, it would have to either avoid the segment or develop capabilities to serve the segment in a way that is better than its competitors. Conversely, the retailer can almost certainly serve other less attractive segments in a very differentiated way within the organization's capabilities. In that instance, the retailer should adjust the RVP to improve the attractiveness of that segment through strategies such as pricing changes, carrying some different product categories, or advertising.

**FIGURE 2.4**

**Target Segment Selection Matrix**

Power retailers prioritize segments based on segment attractiveness and their ability to serve the segment in a differentiated way.

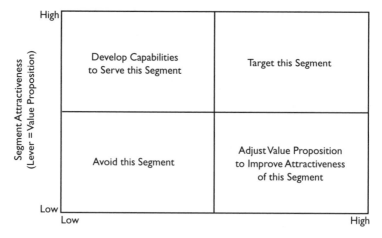

Segmentation is tricky in one other way – it is difficult to recognize a good approach. Power retailers answer the following questions through customer segmentation.

AN INSIDE LOOK

## ALDO SHOES – TARGETING MULTIPLE SEGMENTS

Albert Bensadoun, CEO of Aldo Shoes, used segmentation to target specific groups of customers and dominate the markets in which the company played. That strategy led to the development of six different banners or store names, each targeting its own customer segment, different prices and styles of shoe.

To achieve market dominance, Aldo saturates geographic markets with its storefronts. In Toronto, in the Eaton Centre, there are 17 footwear stores – four of them are Aldo's. Similarly, Aldo has three of 17 footwear stores in the Yorkdale Centre. These stores, representing each of Aldo's banners, are necessary for Aldo to attract different segments, such as high-fashion or price-conscious, within the mall. "This is the key to serving the market well and preventing competition from infiltrating," said Bensadoun. "If there is a good mall, try to have all of the concepts in the mall."

1. *What are the most attractive segments?* How does the market split up into distinct groups, and how does each rank on:
   - size and growth potential (expected future, not historical)
   - cost to serve each segment
   - loyalty to any one retailer's offering
   - lifetime value to the retailer
2. *In what specific, identifiable segments do we make, and lose money?* What products do these groups purchase, and how does this "basket" compare to what other segments buy? Where do we have opportunities to grow the bottom line by increasing our share within certain segments?
3. *Who is our competition?* Where else do these segments shop for goods and services that they could be buying from us? What share do we have in each of the segments, and where are we best positioned and worst positioned?
4. *Why do the different segments shop our store?* What are we offering that is differentially better (or worse, for that matter) than the competition? Is it convenience, experience, prices, selection, or something else?

## Summary

Power retailers use needs-based segmentation as a first step on the way to developing a successful retail strategy. They know that they can't be all things to all people, and choose instead to be number one in the minds and wallets of their specific, identifiable customer segments. They focus on the most attractive segments, which buy high-margin goods, are loyal, and are, or can be, attracted to the retailer's offering.

It is just as important here to determine what not to do as it is to figure out what to do. The retailer who has relied on a loss-leader pricing strategy must deduce whether this adds to or takes away from the target segment's perceived value of the shopping experience. If the loss leader is bulky, clutters the aisles, and isn't purchased by the target convenience customers, then perhaps it attracts a different segment at the expense of the target segment, and should be rethought. Moreover, segmentation may be the foundation of a winning RVP, but to be fully useful it must be combined with information about what the competition is doing. Sometimes getting data about these issues is just as complicated and difficult as doing good segmentation.

**AN INSIDE LOOK**

### PHARMASAVE – REVAMPED STRATEGY

Pharmasave, a 157-store drug chain, with $500 million in sales, primarily in Western Canada, has revamped its strategy based on segmentation.

Through an effective segmentation exercise the company realized that women constituted 85% of their target customer base. The first round of segmentation resulted in data that was too broad since this definition could easily be replaced with "half the human population in Canada are our customers." Another round of segmentation further split this group into two: one driven by needs, the other by "wants." The first category of customers wanted to get in and out of the store quickly and their purchases fell into the "needs" category of products such as toothpaste, shaving accessories, deodorants, and shampoos.

"Everybody chases the needs," says Bond. "Needs products do not generate customer loyalty and they very much lead to the margins game. We wanted to focus on the 'wants' group, which to us represented higher margins, bigger branding opportunity, and would ultimately lead to customer loyalty. We wanted to turn our stores into a destination and decided that 80% of our offering should cater to the 'licence to linger' group."

Consequently, the company chose to shift its focus from the commodity to the value-added product lines. That meant focusing on home health, vitamins, herbal supplements, and high-margin over-the-counter products. The company also decided to branch into services, an area with a decidedly higher profit margin.

Pharmasave's commitment to the new strategy and a laser-like focus led the company to a new slogan, "Live well at Pharmasave," which redefined its drug store business as the wellness business.

"We were looking at 12 relationship categories and wanted to appeal to a given customer, soul and passion. We live in a high-tech society today and people want a high-touch shopping experience," says Bond. "The data from our segmentation exercise made us realize that customers want more than just buying a product, they want internal connections with the product, brand, store staff, and surrounding environment. We set out to create these connections." Pharmasave decided to revamp the inventory, increasing "relationship" product categories, and designed a new look for its stores with a carefully considered layout to appeal to the target customer group.

The design of Pharmasave's stores centred around a colour-coordinated ambience focusing on health and well-being. The aisles were marked with signs that read "wellness," "beauty," and "feel-good," describing the products in terms of what they could do for the customers. For example, a greeting card section, which was extended to include artificial flowers and gifts, welcomes shoppers under the heading of "Celebration Area." This more personal touch extended into training the staff in not just pointing the customer in the general direction of product location but in giving advice about the products' usage and benefits.

Pharmasave saw the results of its strategy fairly quickly. Within 4 to 16 months, depending on the store and its location, the company saw a payback on the remodelling. Right away the new strategy bolstered by thoughtful segmentation resulted in a two-point profit margin lift with the average volume being up 15 to 25%.

# Segmenting Book Buyers

Of 29 million Canadians, market research had indicated that four million of them were potential serious book buyers. These were individuals spending $100 or more on books per year. It was this four million that Chapters planned to target and pamper.

The biggest driver of book-buying patterns was not disposable income, but higher education. Fleshing in the profile further, Chapters' clientele tended to be consumers of the arts. They subscribed to the symphony and attended dramatic arts festivals, art museums, and science exhibitions. By definition, their love of books inferred that they read newspapers and magazines. If they read the *Globe and Mail*, *The National Post*, or *Maclean's*, they were viewed as likely Chapters' customers.

Even though Chapters knew its average customer, Harry Yanowitz, President and Chief Operating Officer comments, "There is no such entity as an 'average' customer. Each customer is unique, and we needed to have a greater understanding of book buyers." A more distilled segmentation process was still required to define, and then target, the Chapters customer more specifically. At that point, the different kinds of stores could expand on their individual strengths.

## The Initial Segmentation Study

Chapters retained Bain & Company in 1994 and 1995 to conduct an exhaustive study of book buyers in Canada. Chapters worked on comprehensive customer surveys, trying to ascertain through store exit interviews the hierarchy of attractiveness of each of the four kinds of stores in its portfolio. These were the airport/Central Business District stores, the mall store, the street-front small store, and the large-format store. At the time of the merger, Chapters had only two large-format stores, one in Montreal and one in Toronto.

Before these initial surveys were completed, it was unknown which selection criteria were most important to patrons of the four different outlets. The criteria evaluated were selection, service and ambience, price, and convenience.

Each of the four store types was found to offer particular strengths that played to customer perceptions. Large-format stores offered the most

## THE FOUR DIFFERENT KINDS OF STORES
## AND THEIR ATTRACTIONS

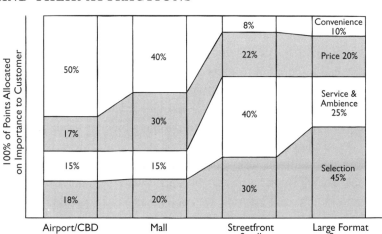

obvious main attraction: enormous selection. Customers said they also expected staff expertise and some discount prices, and enjoyed the plush seating, sequestered and open reading areas, and ready access to the café (many Canadian book buyers' only experience with this format had been in the U.S.).

Street-front small bookstores scored highest in service. Since these stores weren't nearly as sizeable as the large-format venues, staff were considered all the more visible and accessible. Customers said they expected better service, accepting a tradeoff in the smaller selection and higher prices.

Mall stores were found most appealing for their proximity to other shopping, such as Sears, The Gap, and other specialty mall retailers. Convenience was critical, along with customers' perceptions that they were getting good prices. Ambience and selection were not valued nearly as highly as the main draw of convenient one-stop shopping.

Customers of the airport/CBD (central business district) stores were confirmed as the most convenience-driven for the reason that such stores are the only option onsite. Price, service, and selection took a back seat to the ready presence of bookstores at these locations as time-pressed shoppers needed a book quickly.

## *The Next Step: Detailed Segmentation*

The first cut was not designed to capture the broader universe of the retail market, those who did not already shop at Chapters' four types of stores.

Bain & Company completed a deeper analysis based on interviews with several hundred customers and non-customers of Chapters. The newspapers they read, the bookstores they preferred, their general book- and magazine-buying habits were all examined. The intent was to comprehend contrasts between Chapters' shoppers and non-shoppers to discover approaches that Chapters might still incorporate into its retail plan.

All of the amassed information was then divided into designated types of book buyers. The new survey overlapped with Chapters' original segmentation study, while implying ways of reaching newly specified potential customers.

Four kinds of buyers were designated in the book-consuming universe in this segmentation study: the Boutique Buyers, the Impulse Mall Shoppers, the Browsers, and the Bargain Hunters.

## TOTAL MARKET SEGMENTATION
### % of Total Market

| | 38% | 32% | 16% | 14% |
|---|---|---|---|---|

| "Boutique Buyers" | "Impulse Mall Shoppers" | "Browsers" | "Bargain Hunters" |
|---|---|---|---|

Boutique Buyers: Other 20%, Smith/Coles 20%, Independent Bookstores 60%

Impulse Mall Shoppers: Other 55%, Smith/Coles 45%

Browsers: Other 65%, Smith/Coles 35%

Bargain Hunters: Other 75%, Smith/Coles 25%

## CUSTOMER SEGMENTATION:
## COMPETITOR TARGET SEGMENT

| Boutique Buyers | Impulse Mall Shopper | Browsers | Bargain Hunter |
|---|---|---|---|

| **Drivers:** | • Ambience/image | • Convenience | • Selection | • Price |
|---|---|---|---|---|
| | • Selection | • Not service driven | | • Not convenience driven |
| | • Location/service | • Location | | |

"Boutique buyers" demanded the most knowledgeable service. They valued trained staff, and spent more dollars per month than any other customer segment in independent bookstores. As David Hainline, Senior Vice-President – Marketing, Merchandising and Purchasing, explains, "Boutique buyers said in the research that they preferred smaller stores but we interpreted this to be a desire for superior selection and service." At the time this research was conducted, good independent bookstores were the primary outlets delivering this kind of service and selection. The question quickly became how to target and service this largest and most attractive customer segment.

The "impulse mall shoppers" bought books as they caught their eye. They were seen to love shopping malls, while not perceiving that small stores delivered better service. They were unwilling to travel for bargains, and refused to pay more for better service. Chapters found that many of its own mall-store customers were of this group. "Impulse mall shopper" wasn't seen to mean that they only shopped in malls, although mall shoppers were prototypical of this segment. They obviously liked convenience and books, but they weren't willing to drive to a warehouse club to save two dollars. Chapters, through its Coles and SmithBooks stores, had a strong market share in this customer segment, which made it clear the company was already capitalizing on convenience.

The third segment, the "browsers," were those who would rather browse in bookstores more than almost anything else in the world. A discount bookstore, a used bookstore, a large-format store, it didn't matter.

These were individuals who could rarely pass a window full of books without going inside. Chapters also scored well in this group, mainly because the company had the greatest number of stores in which to browse.

The "bargain hunters" were those who were willing to drive across town to save two dollars on a book. Their principle concern was price, and their venues of choice were Costco, Loblaws, Zellers, Wal-Mart, and other non-traditional bookstores. This group of very bargain-sensitive shoppers rarely patronized retail bookstores, and represented the smallest portion of the market.

Each of these four segments had its own cluster of drivers that motivated the book buyers. Each had its own likes and dislikes, driven by personal values and interests. The boutique buyer felt the strongest pull towards bookstores with the greatest selection, traditionally independents. The impulse mall-shopper prized convenience above everything else, and gravitated to mall stores for their ready convenience and proximity to other shopping.

While these stores offered convenience but not necessarily price breaks, grocery stores and discounters offered both convenience and price for the bargain hunters shopping there for groceries and housewares anyway. The browsers were drawn primarily to mall stores and independents, given the proliferation of these book outlets.

Once Chapters had completed the segmentation study, it became much easier to visualize its game plan. Management's aim was to attract the largest and most attractive customer segment by offering the greatest selection while featuring good value. As David Hainline says, "In launching Chapters superstores we were clearly targeting the two most attractive customer segments – the boutique buyers and the browsers."

Building more small stores was not an option, since such a plan wouldn't fill the fundamental gap that existed in the book-retail universe. Only one approach could: large-format stores. It was clear that an opening existed for a new chain of such stores that offered a breadth of selection unknown in Canada.

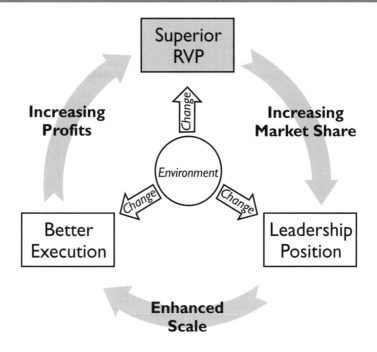

## PRINCIPLE 1:

### Deliver a Customer-driven Superior Retail Value Proposition

*Chapter 2:* THE BASIS FOR STRATEGY—CUSTOMER SEGMENTATION

1. Needs-based segmentation is the critical first step in designing a differentiated RVP.

2. More attractive segments include those which buy high-margin products, are growing, have a lower cost to serve, are loyal, and are predisposed to a retailer's existing RVP.

3. Power retailers make the difficult tradeoffs required to dominate their target segments.

*Chapter 3:* THE ESSENCE OF RETAIL DIFFERENTIATION – THE RETAIL VALUE PROPOSITION

1. The retail value proposition is the promise made to customers about what they can expect from the retailer. This promise is the essence of the brand.

2. The RVP is the benefits including selection, customer experience, and convenience that a retailer delivers in exchange for the price paid.

3. Power retailers choose one of the four elements of RVP on which to excel as the core of their differentiation strategy, while still offering acceptable levels of performance in the remaining three.

# 3 The Essence of Retail Differentiation – The Retail Value Proposition

*"We had to make a choice: to be a commodity retailer going up against the grocery stores, discounters, and mass merchants on price, or to be a value-added retailer that offers fun, high-touch and wants-satisfaction. We figured there was more margin in value-added and a greater chance to be a winner."*

— Brad Bond, CEO, Pharmasave

In Chapter Two we began our look at the first principle for power retailers – developing a clear understanding of market segmentation, identifying attractive segments, and choosing the right target customer. In this chapter, we explore the second part of the first principle; that is, that power retailers offer a competitively superior retail value proposition (RVP). To decide what RVP to offer, retailers consider what their competitors are offering and then what their own organizations can do and want to do. In this chapter, we will discuss the elements of RVP and how power retailers develop a compelling RVP that leads to superior performance.

One way to think about RVP is to equate it to the retail "brand" or identity, that is, what the retailer stands for in the marketplace. Power retailers have clearly defined RVPs, so much so that the power retailer's brand name – such as Wal-Mart, Canadian Tire, Loblaws – evokes in its customers an instinctive, enduring understanding of that retailer's RVP. The perceived RVP is so intrinsic a part of the retailer's identity that customers can correctly articulate the retailer's strategic focus – and this obvious distinctiveness leads to the retailer's superior performance.

## RVP – The Core of Retail Strategy

The RVP is the "package of benefits," the value offering, that a retailer delivers to its customers. In other words, the RVP is what the retailer offers its customers in exchange for their money, time, effort, and loyalty. In our survey of retail CEOs and our observations over the years, we have concluded that the RVP is comprised of four main categories:

1. selection
2. customer experience
3. price
4. convenience

We asked the CEOs in our survey to tell us what aspects of their value offering they felt their customers rated as most important when choosing between their stores and their competitors'. Figure 3.1 summarizes our findings:

In order to provide value, all retailers must deliver some measure of each of these RVP dimensions to customers. Overall, the retail champions tend to exceed customers' minimum threshold on every RVP dimension, but significantly these winners choose to focus on, and are superlative in, delivering *one* particular RVP dimension. Of course, they also deliver the other dimensions of the RVP, but in varying degrees to the primary focus, whether it be selection, customer experience, price, or convenience. Each power retailer picks one dimension to elevate over the other three.

For the power retailers, the key to competitive advantage resides in their ability to differentiate their RVP from their competitors' RVPs. The adage "a retailer must stand for something" goes to the heart of the issue of differentiation in a market of innumerable choices. David Stewart, CEO of Marks & Spencer

**FIGURE 3.1**

### RVP Element

Retail executives ranked selection and customer experience
as most important to their customers.

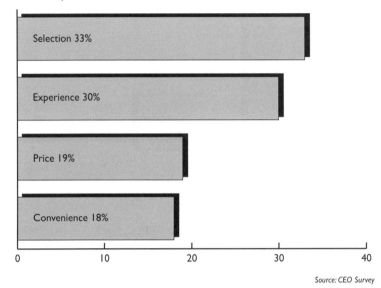

Source: CEO Survey

Canada and formerly CEO of UCS (formerly United Cigar
Store), summed up a lifetime of retail experience on this issue
as follows: "After defining a target audience, the starting point is
finding a point of real, unique, protectable differentiation."
Power retailers have store brands that are meaningful, and they
have RVPs that make a difference in how and where customers
shop. Over the long term, they have built their retail brands in
a strong, consistent fashion that appeals to their target-customer
segments.

As we discussed in Chapter 1 in our quantitative analysis
of retail performance, we examined the Return on Net Assets
(RONA) across three RVP categories: low relative competitive
advantage in RVP, medium relative advantage, and high relative
advantage. As Figure 3.2 shows, RONA was significantly less at
(3.0%) average in the low RVP group relative to the 15% average
in the high RVP group.

FIGURE 3.2

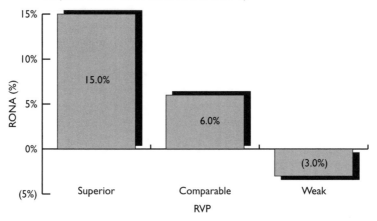

**RONA by RVP**
RVP-superior retailers earned 15% RONA,
compared to RVP-weak retailers that lost money.

Source: Canada Disclosure; S&P Stock Prices; Hoover's Online; OneSource; Annual Reports

The power retailers that outperform their peers know it is not possible to excel on all four dimensions in the marketplace, as the inherent conflict among the four elements inevitably requires making tradeoffs. For example, the retailer that adds convenience will usually have to increase costs, which in turn puts pressure on prices. Because of the need to balance trade-offs, the power retailers find a particular blend of the four RVP elements that their target consumers find not only attractive but compelling. And it's inevitably a mix that their competitors have difficulty matching.

For the customer, value (RVP) is a ratio between the perceived benefits offered by the retailer (selection, experience, convenience) and the perceived cost exacted from the customer (price paid). Consider Costco. This successful wholesale club chain focuses on price at the expense of selection, experience, and convenience. Each Costco unit is located to serve a very large population area, so generally customers must travel some distance to shop there. Once there, they walk great distances across vast parking lots for the privilege of showing their membership card to gain access. In the bare-bones warehouse unit, they search huge floor areas for items on their own with no staff to assist. Decor is non-existent and the larger size packages (designed for wholesale use) are not convenient for many consumers for household use. At the checkout lines, which in peak periods may be very long, customers must produce hard cash, debit cards, or cheques. Credit cards are not accepted. Customers have to pack their own purchases in the used boxes available in the bins that day. And once they've packed up their purchases, they must then pass through security flourishing their receipts to gain exit and carry or push the goods out to their cars. What is the attraction? Above all else, these customers appreciate the low prices.

> *Power retailers have store brands that are meaningful, and they have RVPs that make a difference in how and where customers shop.*

### RVP Formula

$$RVP = \frac{Selection + Experience + Convenience}{Price\ Paid}$$

While this schematic is presented in simple terms, its power is not realized until it is elaborated by segment.

Each RVP factor should actually be portrayed by segment, and represented in a more elaborate fashion. More accurately, the formula would be, as an example, for Segment A, Selection would be expressed as: (Importance of selection to Segment A) X (How well doing on selection relative to competition as perceived by segment A) and Experience would be expressed as: (Importance of experience to Segment A) X (How well doing on selection relative to competition as perceived by segment A), and so on, for each of the four RVP factors in the formula.

## The RVP Components

We now turn to looking at the strategies power retailers employ, for each of the four RVP components.

## ▪ *1. Selection*

We define the selection component of RVP more broadly than the traditional view of the assortment of products for sale. Selection also includes the services that a retailer sells or provides.

Of course, for those retailers that focus on another dimension of the RVP, selection is still a major element of their overall RVP. For all retailers, selection has a major impact on its requirements for its physical facilities and the nature of its sales and marketing efforts as well as the financial model for the business. Stephen Bachand, President and CEO of Canadian Tire, recalls his approach to selection: "We re-examined every category, every linear foot of our stores to decide on our best selection. We determined which categories we needed to dominate, which ones we needed to be competitive in, and which ones we would be convenient in."

Traditionally, many retailers have approached selection in terms of variety, breadth, and depth. Variety refers to the various groups, classes, and categories of items carried. Breadth of selection refers to the selection within each group, class, and category. Whether the retailer's strategy is to offer a wide or narrow selection, breadth determines its number of stock keeping-units (SKUs) but not the quantity. Depth of selection involves the inventory commitment that the retailer makes to a product category; that is, a shallow or deep strategy will determine how many of each SKU a retailer carries. However, in today's competitive economy, this traditional way of thinking about selection is no longer sufficient. In our research on leading retailers, two winning strategies for those focusing on selection consistently emerged: dominant assortment and proprietary products.

### Dominant Assortment

A major selection strategy employed by power retailers is a dominant assortment. This entails having so much selection choice that customers view the retailer as *the* place to go for products in the category in which it is competing. Many retailers choose to dominate through offering breadth and depth in one or more product categories. Often labeled "category-killers," these retailers carry an exceptionally large selection of products. For example, since its opening of its first two stores in 1987, PETsMART has expanded to over 500 superstores in the United States, Canada, and the United Kingdom. In offering more than 12,000 items, its dominant selection strategy dwarfs the small, usually independent, pet food stores.

The Container Store was envisioned from the outset in 1978 as a store that would offer its customers a dominant selection of "solutions to their organization and storage problems." With an average annual growth of 25%, The Container Store clearly demonstrates the power of its unique concept. Each of its 19 superstores offers a staggering array of 12,000 ideas and products (many of them proprietary and many derived from commercial products) for the customer who wants to get organized: shelving, filing systems, desk organizers, shoe racks, CD holders, bottles and bags, closet organizers, and many other storage problem-solvers.

Dominant selection sometimes requires a bigger floor plate, but the actual size needed for dominance is relative to what the other competitors in the category have. The average size of a PETsMART store is 25,000 square feet – small in comparison to today's big-box format but certainly much larger than its competitors' stores. On the other hand, in the home improvement sector, Home Depot's stores average 110,000 square feet, which allows them to be the dominant leader in selection, offering 40,000 to 60,000 items, four times as many as most of its competitors.

*For all retailers, selection – the range of products and the services a retailer offers – has a major impact on the retailer's requirements for its physical facilities, the nature of its sales and marketing efforts, and the financial model for the business.*

Whatever the size of the store that focuses on dominant selection, the basic appeal is that customers know that a trip to one store is probably all that is needed to find all of the product offerings in a product category. Sometimes, dominant selection means

## AN INSIDE LOOK

## AUTONATION – A CAR SUPERSTORE

With North Americans buying 60 million new and used cars a year, the prospect of becoming a dominant retailer for automobiles is very attractive. While manufacturers' franchised dealers have long dominated the new car industry, a highly fragmented, largely independent retail system has developed for used cars in response to market demands. For customers, the used-car salesman brings to mind a negative image and a lot of bad jokes. It is well known that used-car customers hate going from dealer to dealer to find cars and are increasingly disgruntled with the selling process, a process they liken to the horsetrading of yesteryear.

In 1996, Wayne Huizenga, owner of Republic Industries and its subsidiary Blockbuster Video, announced he was building a nationwide network of new- and used-car outlets to consolidate the industry by creating a national brand. In his first six months, he bought 65 auto dealerships with 109 outlets selling 31 brands, opened eleven 1,000-vehicle used-car superstores called AutoNation USA, and bought three rental-car companies, including Alamo and National.

Each of the 26 AutoNation outlets is both a new- and used-car superstore, with huge lots for 1,000 cars and 25,000 square feet of high-tech showroom, rather than the 50 or fewer cars found on most used-car lots. Customers use touch-screen computer kiosks to browse and match up the cars and options they want with the inventory. Knowledgeable "guides," rather than used-car salesmen, are available to help customers in their selection.

AutoNation offers cars at fixed prices and money-back guarantees. Every car sale comes with a seven-day, money-back guarantee, a 99-day warranty, and free roadside assistance for a year. No car is more than five years old. A service centre handles all makes and models and a 2,000-item accessory shop stocks all of the options.

assurance that a desired item will be in stock. For example, Blockbuster Video successfully recognized and corrected an initially weak selection strategy to gain advantage over its competitors. Earnings were down due to less traffic and a decrease in new memberships. In re-examining its selection strategy, management came up with a simple but very effective approach: stock more of the new releases that customers want. As the chain grew in size, its scale allowed it to negotiate deals with the major studios to obtain more copies of new releases than its competitors. Blockbuster now carries three times as many copies of new releases and guarantees its customers that the latest hits will be in stock, or next time they're free.

## Proprietary Products

The power retailers that demonstrate a strong commitment to proprietary selection offer something special, something others in the same sector do not offer. For example, 85% of Victoria's Secret's assortment are its own private-label products, while 75% of Bath & Body Works' selection is their own product. Uniqueness can mean designing and having manufactured an exclusive line that bears the retailer's own label. Marks & Spencer and Sainsbury in the U.K., Sears, Radio Shack, and Canadian Tire – to name a few – have all made significant commitments to private-label programs. Radio Shack has focused its proprietary selection to the point of offering just one brand, its own Realistic brand, and excluding other manufacturers' brands.

Proprietary selection enables a retailer to add to its brand image, to engender loyalty amongst customers who wish to continue buying its exclusive products, to gain higher margins, and to obtain an understanding of the economics of manufacturers' brands. For example, Shoppers Drug Mart has unique products such as its control-labels Life, Health Watch, and Rialto – and a new cosmetic line, QUO. Companies such as Brookstone, Sharper Image, L.L. Bean, and Lee Valley all offer proprietary selections of merchandise that attract customers from great distances.

Oilily is another example of a retailer champion that has prospered with a proprietary selection. This 35-year-old company sells baby clothes, children's clothes, women's wear, perfumes, shoes, accessories and more in 45 countries, ringing up sales of

$175 million in the U.S. alone. The essence of Oilily's success is its unique, imaginative design of children's clothes – colourful, durable clothes with whimsical trimmings such as animal earflaps and wings – clothes that children love to wear. In fact, its children's clothes became so popular that the company successfully added women's wear for the mothers after Oilily discovered that they were trying to squeeze into their kids' clothes.

Almost every retailer can use a blend of national brands and proprietary products to enhance its selection. For example, Safeway (with its Select brand) and J.C. Penney (with its Worthington brand) successfully blend their premium private brands with manufacturer brands in their selection.

## ◼ *2. Customer Experience*

Harry Rosen, Warner Bros., Rainforest Café, and Mountain Equipment Co-op may seem to be very diverse power retailers, but what they all have in common is a focus on the second aspect of the RVP, customer experience. These retailers distinguish themselves not simply by the products they offer, but how shoppers experience their visits to the retailer's place of business. Ten million customers buy Starbucks' coffee each week, but Howard Schultz, Chairman and CEO of Starbucks, said: "It is our goal to offer more than just a great cup of coffee – we want to offer a memorable experience."

The experience dimension of RVP encompasses all of the many ways a retailer manages its relationships with its customers beyond the transaction itself. Customer experience is not just what is done for customers to get them in a store and complete a transaction, but also how it is done and what extras are provided. While this RVP dimension includes many ways a retailer can satisfy and delight customers, the power retailers that emphasize this RVP tend to focus on either:

- Care: helpful information, personal attention, and value-added services or
- Entertainment: sensory stimulation and diversions

## AN INSIDE LOOK

## MARS – SELECTION OUT OF THIS WORLD

In the music sector, the MARS superstore is rapidly becoming the musician's choice for both purchases and rentals of all instruments. The guitar-playing former president and CEO of Office Depot Mark Begelman began this business in late 1995 with the purchase of a small four-unit music chain. Following his vision to dominate the musical instrument market, he transformed these into MARS (Music And Recording Superstore). There are now more than 30 MARS units, each with approximately 35,000 square feet and offering a vast selection of virtually every musical instrument – 200,000 SKUs in all – except acoustic pianos or church organs. The staff are all musicians and browsers are encouraged to jam.

The Florida-based superstores attract all musicians, from beginners to pros, with rentals and sales, music lessons, installations of sound systems, and in-store performances. By way of comparison, the typical musical instrument retail business has long been characterized by 600- to 2,000-square-foot independent stores that specialize in only a few instruments.

**Care**

Care is a broader concept than customer service. Customer-care relates to the retailer's respect for customers and is evident in the information provided to help the customer make shopping decisions, the personal attention available, and the value-added services provided.

Christine Magee, President of Sleep Country Canada, outlines her customer-care vision this way: "When a customer comes in our door we want to exceed their expectations. We want them to have a fun experience. We want to educate them on their own sleep needs. We don't let our sales associates make a sale until they have had three to four weeks' training, including visits to the factories. We can't fix a bad back, but we can help customers by asking certain questions to find what mattress is best for them. We aren't selling mattresses and box springs; we're selling a good night's sleep."

## ROOTS – PROPRIETARY SELECTION

Established in 1973, Roots is a manufacturer and retailer of "athletic-inspired high-quality leather products and casual clothing for men, women and children," which began with one proprietary product, the negative heel "earth" shoe. There are 95 Roots stores in Canada, six in the U.S., and 13 in the Pacific Rim markets of Taiwan, Korea, Hong Kong, and Japan. Roots has expanded its proprietary line from leather shoes, bags, jackets, and accessories to the addition of Baby and Kids clothing in 1982, athletic wear in 1985, and most recently, the introduction of Roots Time, a line of licensed watches, and Roots Vision, a line of eyewear and sunglasses launched in 1995. Ninety-five per cent of Roots goods are made in Canada, of which the majority are made in the Roots wholly-owned factories in Toronto. The place to buy a Roots jacket is at Roots. Roots was extraordinarily visible at the 1998 Olympic Games in Nagano when athletes and countless others sported the Roots bright red Canadian berets and clothing designed for the event.

Customers value relevant information because it saves them time, effort, and money. Power retailers respond to this need with catalogues, flyers, customer newsletters, product fact sheets, Internet home pages, displays, informative signage in the store itself, and, of course, trained and knowledgeable sales staff. For example, IKEA's catalogues and its interactive Web site help customers plan their rooms before they even enter their stores. Like other power retailers that follow this strategy, IKEA builds on its better understanding of what its customers want and need to know and when they want to know. Restoration Hardware provides interesting product anecdotes on cards for their unusual selection of household items.

Some customers highly value personal interaction with the retailer's people. Harry Rosen is clearly a retailer for these customers. As he says, "Our mission is to exceed each customer's expectations. That means we have to have the most professional staff and highest quality service possible. It means we have to support our people with state-of-the-art information systems. And it means we train people all the time." They want salespeople to help them make selections, provide product information, find ways to customize the product or service just for them and generally make them feel good about their decision to buy.

Traditionally retailers have offered, and continue to offer, extra services that complement the products they sell – Sears provides store credit and delivers to the customer's home, Holt Renfrew provides gift-wrapping services, Peoples Jewellers cleans their customers' jewellery for free. In offering additional services that their customers value, some retailers set up a piggyback arrangement with a franchise or smaller independent that benefits both businesses.

**Entertainment**

A rapidly growing strategy, and perhaps more aptly termed "retailtainment," entertainment is found in unusual displays and props, interactive games, video walls, rides for children – and even indoor beaches, water slides, and submarine rides such as found at the West Edmonton Mall. Sometimes entertainment involves giving customers fun yet practical opportunities to try equipment under realistic conditions. The shower area in Bata's Out There stores gives customers an opportunity to test outerwear in the rain just as the climbing walls in Mountain Equipment Co-op stores (and its U.S. equivalent REI) let customers test climbing shoes and equipment. Similarly, BassPro's testing pool for fly rods and its archery range allow customers to enjoy the product before purchase.

Sometimes entertainment consists of sensory stimulation and sometimes entertainment consists of more elaborate diversions. Power retailers use sensory stimulation to make the shopping experience less onerous and more fun. For example, in creating environments that please the senses, the latest versions of upscale kitchen furnishings retailer Williams Sonoma lure customers with cooking smells venting into the corridors of malls. Great retailers involve all of the senses, knowing that atmosphere and surroundings affect customers psychologically and physiologically and ultimately can encourage shoppers to make purchases. Knowing the

AN INSIDE LOOK

## NORDSTROM – DO THE LITTLE THINGS RIGHT

The leader in its sector, the U.S. Nordstrom department store chain offers its customers a unique and tremendous product selection in fashion for men and women, but its key point of differentiation is its outstanding customer care. Nordstrom does the little things right.

Nordstrom does not compete on price; it delivers superior customer care and experience right down to the finest detail. To keep customers happy while trying on clothes, each changing room is equipped with its own thermostat. The changing rooms are also large enough to accommodate toddlers and strollers. Of course, these and other customer-driven features add costs, but the costs are justified in its delivery of a superior RVP that in turn sustains its outstanding financial performance.

In keeping with this RVP strategy, Nordstrom's employees, affectionately referred to as "Nordies," are arguably the best salespeople in the business. They are also the best-paid employees in the business. Through its merit program, Nordstrom awards the top 8 to 12% of salespeople in each division with the "Pacesetter" status and an opportunity to earn in excess of $100,000 annually. Of course, the culture is such that salespersons who cannot deliver extraordinary service will actually decide to leave on their own accord. In 1998, Nordstrom was ranked the top retailer in the American Customer Satisfaction Index with a score of 82, just short of the overall top performer, Mercedes-Benz, with its score of 87.

After many year of double-digit profit growth, Nordstrom expanded rapidly in the 1990s and suffered a severe earnings drop in 1997; however, sales and profits recovered dramatically in 1998. As of 1999, Nordstrom management is converting the manual clientele system to an on-line version to assist its sales associates in delivering the care Nordstrom has been known for.

power of atmosphere, the power retailers entice customers with interesting exhibits, exciting, unusual store design, and dramatic visual merchandising. Banana Republic, a division of The Gap, is known for its delightful fantasy interiors, as is Victoria's Secret for its femininely seductive decor. On the other hand, Crate & Barrel offers an attractive, clean, contemporary look in its stores, while FAO Schwarz is abuzz with excitement. Home Depot offers in-store demos for children on how to build birdhouses.

Annette Verschuren, President of Home Depot, puts it this way: "It is a privilege to have customers come into our stores. We are in the entertainment business and we are on stage every minute of every day." Just as the set and costumes are vital to a theatre production and music and soft lighting enhance a fine meal, some retailers have gained a competitive edge by stage-managing the retail theatre in which they operate.

Some power retailers compete with diversions that are expensive and high-tech, such as the 3-D movies on the top floor of Warner Bros. Studio Store in New York. Others add excitement to the shopping trip with surprising decor or events. Toronto's discounter, Honest Ed's, surprises and delights its customers with its outrageous decor, humorous promotions, and well-publicized charitable events such as the Christmas turkey giveaway it stages each year.

## AN INSIDE LOOK

### DISCOVERY CHANNEL – INFO-TAINMENT

Sometimes entertainment is in fact "info-tainment." For example, the Washington, D.C., flagship store of Discovery Channel, a $20-million 30,000-square-foot store, is a museum, movie theatre, interactive game arcade, and a media centre. As customers enter the front door, they're greeted with a 36-screen 270-degree video and audio presentation area that displays clips from some of Discovery Channel's programs. Attractions include the largest T-Rex skeleton ever assembled (42 feet long), the forward fuselage of a B-25 bomber, an 8-foot cave bear skeleton, and a giant ant colony. The mezzanine level is designed to look like the inside of a ship complete with underwater bubbles outside the windows. Much of the store is interactive, allowing customers to identify plane types on radar, watch videos and sample music at watching/listening stations, and create sand dunes with a wind machine or simulate Saturn clouds on another device. Even the elevator ride, with its unique decor, is worth a store visit.

## RETAIL-TAINMENT STORIES – THE NBA STORE, RAINFOREST CAFÉ, AND MARS 2112

### The NBA Store

During the fall of 1998, the National Basketball Association was off the court because of a labour dispute with players. But that didn't stop the launch of its superstore in New York City. Two storeys high and stocked with over 15,000 products, the NBA Store is the first retail establishment owned, operated, and merchandised by a North American sports league. With 57 million adult basketball fans in the United States, the NBA Store has a large and potentially very profitable customer base.

The NBA Store gives customers an experience unlike that of any traditional retail store. Customers enter through a limestone archway and walk down ramps with flashing scoreboards overhead, to the lower-level retail area. The store is part museum, part media centre, and part store. Customers can visit broadcasting booths, sit on the bleachers to watch coaching clinics and demonstrations on the basketball half-court, or settle in at the media centre to watch tapes of the NBA's 50-year history and live-game broadcasts. And while they're being entertained, customers can buy licensed NBA merchandise and even have some items customized while they wait.

### Rainforest Café

The chain of Rainforest Café restaurants was founded in 1994 to capitalize on the growing popularity of restaurants like Planet Hollywood and the Hard Rock Café. Now expanded to 18 units, the Rainforest Café recently reported gross revenues of over $100 million.

With its live parrots, animatronic animals, exotic simulated rainforest setting, and environmentalist theme, it claims to be "a wild place to shop and eat." These restaurants are designed to appeal to all of the senses; in fact, some patrons observing their children's distraction from eating might even say they overstimulate the senses.

In 1997, Rainforest Café won an industry-sponsored NRN (National Retail Federation) Hot Concepts! Award and received plaudits for its operations at Disney theme parks. In 1998, it entered the Canadian market, opening its first Rainforest Café in Burnaby, British Columbia.

**Mars 2112**

Mars 2112, "the galaxy's first intergalactic restaurant," opened a $15 million startup location in Times Square in 1998. While diners wait for their tables, they can visit the Star Bar to watch the Martian TV news and weather forecasts while the children play in the game area called Cyberstreet. From there, diners travel on a space shuttle ride to the restaurant situated in a crater below the surface of Mars. Throughout the meal, patrons are entertained with flying spaceships, space trains, and meteor showers. Live theatre scenes such as a spaceship hijacking, an oxygen equipment emergency, and a visit by the Martian empress amuse diners.

Those power retailers who compete using the entertainment factor are attracting the time-constrained and tired shoppers who appreciate the fun and leisure they can find there. Entertainment may keep shoppers in the store or at the Web site longer by amusing, informing, and stimulating, which in the end can drive superior retail performance. But the stakes can be high. After all, entertainment is expensive to provide. If not carefully developed as part of the overall RVP strategy, entertainment can become too diversionary and get in the way of the prime purpose of the retailer – to sell merchandise. This pitfall is perhaps most visible in the restaurant sector where some of the new theme eateries have focused so much on "eater-tainment," they seem to have forgotten the food. This deficiency, combined with huge up-front costs and too-rapid expansion that reduces the uniqueness and novelty of the customer experience, has resulted in significant year-two same-store (comparable stores) sales declines, and thus poor financial performance in this segment of the casual restaurant industry. Planet Hollywood's shares, once traded at $25, dropped to just over $1 in 1999. Rainforest Café's shares have fallen nearly 70% between May 1998 and May 1999.

Diversions provide a fun quotient, but they can require a heavy investment in such things as stage design, sound and projection systems, sets, props, and even additional staffing. And as the novelty soon wears thin, shoppers will inevitably move on to find something new and better in entertainment, a trend that continually raises the bar for the "fun quotient" in the shopping experience.

### ◼ *3. Price*

A third dimension of RVP that a retailer might emphasize is price. Retailers continually debate the many issues surrounding pricing. Some options are strategic, such as everyday low pricing, and some are tactical, such as familiar and unfamiliar price endings. Those power retailers who compete primarily on price generally do so on "lowest pricing."

While all retailers may reduce their prices from time to time, some retailers, as a matter of strategy, *always* price below the market – these are the discounters. Discounters come in many forms – wholesale/warehouse clubs, deep discounters, catalogue showrooms, liquidators, off-pricers, dollar stores, hypermarkets, and superstores. The discounters (such as Zellers and Wal-Mart), off-pricers (such as Winners, TJMaxx, and BiWay), warehouse clubs (such as Costco and Sam's), and the "extreme value retailers" (such as Family Dollar and Dollar General) all have a primary focus on the price dimension of the RVP. These retailers gain and hold a competitive edge with sharp pricing such as special limited time prices, everyday low prices, or automatically declining prices.

These types of retailers rely on buying items less expensively than their direct competitors, selling higher volumes, achieving higher turnover rates, and creating a lower cost structure. They also reduce their offerings on the other dimensions of RVP to save costs. The discounters cater to a large segment of the population, not just those that have lower incomes. Today's price-sensitive customer is not necessarily economically downscale.

Off-price retailers offer from 20 to 40% off the prices that the conventional retailers charge for the same goods. For example, Winners carries a limited number of apparel SKUs with a focus on high turnover, high volume. Overhead is low because the stores are located in less costly facilities and offer few amenities. The inventory ranges from last-season and surplus to this season,

## AN INSIDE LOOK

### COSTCO COMPANIES – COMPETING ON LOWEST PRICE

In 1976, Sol Price began an experiment in discount retailing that was to have a profound impact on the retail industry. Like many retail innovations, this one began in Southern California. He opened a store called Price Club in San Diego, California, as a membership store for wholesale customers only. After a disappointing start, Price broadened his operation to include regular retail customers, although the wholesale customer eventually proved to be the most profitable segment for this concept.

Price perceived that small-business customers in particular were not being well served by conventional wholesalers. He reasoned that these customers purchased more often and in far greater quantities than retail customers. Accordingly, his concept was built on limited assortment (3,600 to 4,000 products), high volume, and low margin. Price Club became the prototype for what are now called wholesale clubs, warehouse clubs, and membership clubs. During the '80s, wholesale clubs proliferated, but by the end of the decade, there had been a major shakeout and consolidation in the industry, prompting two of the three leading firms, Price Club and Costco, to merge into Costco Companies, Inc. As of 1999, Costco Companies is the largest wholesale club operator in the U.S. (ahead of Wal-Mart's Sam's Club), with about 300 membership warehouse stores serving 27 million members in the eastern and western U.S., Canada, Mexico, South Korea, Taiwan, and the U.K. Costco's 1998 sales of U.S. $24 billion grew 11% over 1997 while net income increased by 47%.

Costco's high inventory turnover allows it to operate on negative inventory investment – that is, the merchandise is sold before the suppliers' bills come due. In effect, the suppliers finance the operation. The savings in inventory, combined with membership, constitute the bulk of Costco's net profits. Costco offers products in large, institutional package sizes or in multiples shrink-wrapped and sold together on floor pallets and warehouse shelving. Items are not individually price-marked. While all customers must be members, retail members pay 5% more than wholesale members. Marketing costs are kept low by restricting advertising and promotion to store openings only. Finally, services are very limited: cash-and-carry with almost no on-floor service help, no credit, and no delivery.

with the emphasis on opportunistic buying of closeouts, end-of-season, slightly damaged, special runs, and so on, all at favourable prices. Of course, the continuity of selection is generally low.

Wholesale clubs are not simply variations on supermarkets and general mass merchandisers, but usually have quite different formats and operations. They achieve their ability to focus on price (typically 20 to 40% below those of other retail outlets) as their dominant RVP factor by situating in large, spartan units in low-cost, out-of-the-way locations, thus reducing real estate costs. They offer a very limited assortment of high brand leaders, typically carrying 3,000 to 5,000 SKUs. Merchandise is bought opportunistically, with more commitment to categories than to particular brands, meaning the costs are low but the continuity spotty. They buy directly and do not warehouse other than right in the store, again reducing costs.

## AN INSIDE LOOK

## ALDI – LOWEST GROCERY PRICES

The grocery sector is a good example of a great variety of pricing strategies, where both lowest prices and credible prices can be successful. The German-based grocer Aldi offers a very limited assortment of dry groceries at the lowest prices in its sector. Aldi (short for all discounts) is Germany's fourth-largest retail organization with over 4,500 "no frills" outlets worldwide.

One of the most successful box stores in Europe, Aldi offers approximately 600 SKUs, far fewer than a typical supermarket's 18,000 to 20,000 SKUs. The stores carry very little fresh produce and no fresh meat or deli items. Aldi only sells items on which it can control the brand, or secondary brands which are lower-priced. Aldi's private-label sales account for 90% of sales. The stores are plain and small, typically 10,000 to 12,000 square feet, and thus are very efficient and can do well on much lower volumes than supermarkets. The stores operate on low prices but do not engage in promotional pricing or price wars. It is a cash-only operation with cut-case displays and no advertising.

Lowest pricing is one of the most challenging strategic positions to take in the retail industry. History shows us that one-time price leaders frequently get underpriced by new competitors and quickly lose their place in the industry. For example, the once price-leading catalogue showrooms with their locked-in catalogue prices have all but disappeared as lower-priced, more nimble discounters have taken their place. To succeed over the long run with the lowest price strategy, management must be extremely vigilant and committed to maintaining a significant cost advantage over all competitors (we go into more detail on this subject in Chapter 6). The remarkable success of Wal-Mart has been attributed to many factors, but its disciplined ability to lower prices over time has been central to their performance – and that has been made possible by a continuous reduction in their costs.

## 4. Convenience

A fourth strategy for developing a winning RVP is convenience. For customers, convenience is often as simple as being able to shop and buy with a minimal expenditure of time and effort. Is a store easy to find, to get to, to park near and to enter, or in the case of the Internet, to access? And when the customer enters, is it easy to find items and information, to complete the transaction and to leave?

All retailers must make decisions on convenience factors, but those retail winners who have focused on the convenience RVP have each raised the bar on convenience in some way. In our survey, we found fewer retailers saying that convenience was their primary RVP than those who said their focus was selection, experience, or price. Customers short of time and older customers represent new opportunities to improve an RVP through added convenience. Even assortment can be looked at through the lens of convenience: too much choice and too little choice in selection are both strategies that waste customers' time.

The most commonly known retailers that make convenience the primary focus of their RVP strategy are the corner "convenience stores" or C-Stores. Once small neighbourhood milk-and-bread stores for fill-in trips between their customers' visits to a

*Convenience-focused power retailers respect their customers' time. Their choices of locations, layout, hours and bundling reflect this dedication.*

supermarket, many of these stores have extended their convenience offerings to include prepared take-out foods, video rentals, postal, photocopying, and fax services, in-store bakeries, ABMs for quick cash, and dry cleaning services. They typify what convenience means: saving the customer time and effort. A leading example in this sector is the Silcorp group. By 1999, Silcorp had grown to be the largest convenience store operator in Canada, with 865 locations in Ontario and Western Canada, operating under the Mac's, Mike's Mart, and Becker's banners.

Of course, all retailers have to address convenience issues regardless of their primary RVP focus. While there are many aspects to convenience, the power retailers consistently focus on either accessibility or speed.

### Accessibility

Power retailers respect their customers' time; they don't waste it. Their choices of locations, layouts, hours, and other access factors reflect the constant tradeoff between saving customers time and saving the retailer money. While in the past retailers focused on their own efficiencies, often at the expense of the customers' efficiency, today's power retailers visibly value their customers' time.

For example, from the customer's perspective, the retailer's location is primarily a convenience issue, whether it is a "bricks-and-mortar" or a virtual store. Of course, for a retailer relying on convenience as a primary RVP, choice of location is critical. The customer segment that values convenience will go to the closest retailer that can meet their needs and wants – and for the most part will not travel past a retailer that satisfies their needs to shop at an equal facility farther away. For example, Home Depot with its large warehouse stores located far apart is now experimenting with a locationally convenient format called Villager's Hardware in New Jersey. Similarly, Staples has launched Staples Express to cater to the customer who values the convenience of location.

Accessibility, of course, includes the hours that a retailer is available for business. The trend in North America is to be open for longer and longer hours – some retailers are open twenty-four hours a day, seven days a week, such as Shoppers Drug Mart's 24 X 7 drug stores. This round-the-clock accessibility has led to a renewed emphasis on vending machines of all kinds. Automatic banking machines and other kinds of electronic kiosks are good examples of retailers finding new ways to offer increased accessibility for customers. Indeed, ABMs are retail kiosks. With their uses growing at an explosive rate, electronic retail kiosks now vend theatre and

*Electronic kiosks of all kinds are proliferating as retailers look for new ways to offer more accessibility and convenience to their customers.*

transportation tickets, stamps, and various other products. For example, Circuit City has installed kiosks in its 520 electronics and appliance stores to improve customer access to computer and appliance manufacturers. Customers can compare prices and different configurations across brands and custom-order products to be delivered directly to their home or to their local store for pickup.

Electronic kiosks will continue to proliferate as retailers engage the many convenience-related features now available. They can now roll an informative video clip, use a camera for a security eye scan, communicate in several languages, process airline tickets, accept donations for charities, and issue gift certificates. In Japan, there are even electronic kiosks that sanitize and press paper currency before vending the bills to the customer.

Time-shifting is another valuable convenience aspect of electronic kiosks as well as of Internet and catalogue retailing. These strategies make the retailers accessible at the customers' convenience, regardless of time, even when traditional retailers are closed. Internet shopping, in particular, offers some unique accessibility values. Customers can deal with retailers in distant locales and avoid dealing with the weather, parking, and traipsing around the store. Selection is vast. With just a few mouse

## CONVENIENCE – GROCERIES ON-LINE

**AN INSIDE LOOK**

According to the Andersen Consulting's 1998 survey of 2,600 consumers, on-line shopping for groceries and household goods is des-
tined to increase dramatically from U.S. $100 million in 1997 to U.S.
$85 billion in 2007. Peapod, Streamline, NetGrocer, and HomeGrocer
are the three major Internet grocers that have set their sights on this
lucrative market, each with a different approach. However, all have
had a difficult startup period and although profits were premised on
meeting the convenience needs of customers, the financial performance of these firms still remains unattractive.

Peapod, which began in 1989 in Chicago, partners with grocery stores, in
effect brokering the relationship with its customers. Peapod offers over
30,000 items to its members. Customers can order by Internet, phone, or
fax. Peapod then has its own shoppers pick items from the shelves of a
local store or warehouse and deliver the order to the customer at a pre-
arranged time. Somebody needs to be home to receive the order. As of
1999, Peapod was switching its approach to serving customers out of a
central warehouse, which cut its cost of fulfillment between 20 to 30 per
cent. For providing this guaranteed shopping convenience, Peapod charges
membership fees, which are based on order size and a delivery fee.

Streamline, which began in 1993 in the Boston area and is now backed
by Nordstrom Inc., uses a consumer resource centre (CRC) to process
orders. This CRC is not a public store, but rather a separate 56,000-square-
foot replenishment facility that provides for warehouse cost efficiencies in
order fulfillment. Streamline's concept is to offer routine replenishment
and delivery of groceries, postage stamps, prepared meals, diapers, dry
cleaning services, photo-processing, and pickups of clothing donations, as
well as video rentals with its partner Blockbuster Video.

Streamline management describes the operation as a grocery delivery
company. While it offers a great variety of goods and services, the number
of grocery items is about one-third of Peapod's offering. However,
Streamline does not require the customer to be home to receive their
deliveries. Streamline can leave a special freezer-size insulated box in the
customer's garage, an arrangement made easier with some Streamline
equity being held by General Electric. Of course, the Streamline trucks are

equipped with refrigeration units and special sections for hanging dry cleaning.

NetGrocer also works from a central warehouse, but ships nationally using Federal Express. NetGrocer's approach leapfrogs Peapod's local market by concentrating on local market growth one market at a time. However, it can only offer non-perishable items, about 3,000 items in all. Rather than partnering with grocery retailers, NetGrocer partnered briefly with America OnLine (AOL). In 1999, NetGrocer management was changed and so was most of the NetGrocer approach. Most observers believe that the higher costs of and longer delays in delivery do not make the NetGrocer method attractive or viable.

HomeGrocer is a newer entrant operating on the U.S. West Coast. Operating much like Streamline, HomeGrocer offers a major difference in its delivery approach. HomeGrocer places special hot/cold lockbox units (disguised as sheds or benches) outside the home for unattended delivery of groceries.

clicks, the customer can access all of a retailer's selection. For customers that require more information about the products, assistance is just another mouse click away – most sites provide valuable information about products and related services.

## Speed

Another important dimension of convenience, speed attracts busy customers who want to find the items they are interested in and complete the transaction and the entire shopping trip quickly. In responding to these needs, power retailers use innovative layout, signs, transaction processes, and home delivery to reduce the time it takes to shop in a physical or virtual store.

As customers want to move through the store quickly, power retailers use layout to speed up customer traffic and improve buying patterns. Of course, with space costs ever increasing, retailers of any size are already pressed to use space as effectively and efficiently as possible.

## WEBER'S – CUSTOMERS LINE UP FOR FAST SERVICE

A take-out hamburger operation located north of Toronto, Ontario, Weber's speeds up transactions by having employees work on the floor right in the customer waiting line. One staff member walks along the line-up asking customers for orders and filling in preprinted forms that cover all the menu options. Another staff member follows up by taking the money and returning change. The order goes to the master cook so that, as the line moves along, the customer's order is ready approximately at the time the customer reaches the take-out counter. The efficiency is so successful that one small unit with one grill can serve up to 900 people per hour at peak times.

The novelty of the approach strikes customers as a sincere attempt to meet their convenience needs. Despite predictable line-ups that can stretch for blocks during the peak cottage season, the customers come back year after year. In fact, customers now consider the line-up part of the fun at Weber's, a welcome break from highway driving. While the kids explore the park-like setting and old railroad car behind the store, the adults chat with fellow cottagers driving north to the lakes. Weber's has become so popular that an overhead pedestrian bridge had to be built across the highway for southbound customers who stopped in on their way home from the cottage.

Delivery has long been a way to offer convenience. Pharmacies such as Walgreen's and Eckerd's are providing drive-through order and pickup windows. Similarly, airlines, car rental firms, dry cleaners, video rental stores, and others now have "express services" to speed up their transactional operations for the time-conscious customer.

Power retailers use a great variety of initiatives to speed up their customers' shopping excursions. They increase staffing for high-volume peak periods as well as make sure all employees receive the training they need to reach optimal efficiency in all procedures. They increase the number of staff who can authorize cheques so the customer doesn't stand waiting for the supervisor to authorize the transaction. They use magnetic-strip readers and automatic dialers for credit card authorization calls. Rather than use the checkout as another sales attempt or market research venue, they only ask customers to provide necessary information. If additional paperwork is necessary to complete a transaction, the cashiers are directed to do this after the transaction rather than on the customer's time. Retailers that take orders by phone and the Internet use on-line customer information so customers are not asked the same questions every time they order. For example, Pizza Pizza has long used telephone numbers as customer identifiers to speed up orders of pizza from repeat customers.

Even retailers whose primary focus is not convenience need to find ways to offer increased convenience. For example, Albertson's, a major regional grocery chain in the southern U.S., has developed dramatically different layouts in its stores based on its careful analysis of shoppers' feedback in ongoing focus group research. Shoppers said they wanted a more logical layout since most of them shop without a list, so Albertson's grouped items together in category centres. Coffee isn't in one place and juice in another and soda pop in yet another; they're all together in the Beverage Center. Ready-to-go food is grouped together in the Meal Center. In other words, the stores group the merchandise in ways that make sense to the customer. To make sure the customers find the centres quickly, Albertson's set up enormous signs over each centre that are visible the moment its customers enter the store. To improve the visibility of products, Albertson's lowered its shelves.

## Summary

The retail value proposition (RVP) is the promise made to customers about what they can expect from the retailer. This promise is the essence of the retailer's brand or identity. RVP is the package of benefits – comprised of selection, customer experience, convenience, and price – that a retailer provides in exchange for the customer's business. All retailers have a blend of these four elements, but power retailers choose one of the four RVP elements at which to excel as the core of their differentiation strategy, while still offering acceptable levels of performance on the remaining three. Power retailers have RVPs that are so distinguishable and compelling that shoppers come again and again, bringing the retailer superior market performance. However, even after carefully matching capabilities with competitive offerings and consumer-needs segments, power retailers do not stand still once they have determined their RVP strategy. As the market changes, they change their RVPs, a topic we will return to in Chapter 8.

---

## Designing the RVP

**THE CHAPTERS' PERSPECTIVE**

Chapters has three retail value propositions: one each for the mall stores, the large-format stores, and the Internet.

### The Mall Stores

Chapters compares the functionality of its mall stores to that of convenience stores. They are strategically placed at the right crossroads, and make it easy for walk-in mall customers to find bestsellers, new releases, and gifts. Selective merchandising makes for quick browsing, quick selling, and fast product turnover. The RVP is *convenience*.

### The Internet

The Net adds new dimensions to book-buying: at-home, leisurely browsing, and an unimaginably broad selection of over three million titles. As Rick Segal, President of Chapters Internet, points out, "We often have 1,000 Canadians visiting our site at 2:00 a.m. when all of our stores are closed." The RVP is *selection* and *convenience*.

### The Superstore

In Chapters' view, customer expectations are set by what its management calls the "universal experience" – that is, all customers' experiences. Chapters makes the point of trying to learn from everybody, not just booksellers. As Dan Soper, Senior Vice-President of Large-Format Stores, points out, "We want to be the best service provider in the world, like the Four Seasons Hotels, and we use other outstanding companies as our benchmarks." The company's wide scope naturally led to its having the broadest possible vision of what the best buying experience would be for its own clientele.

Industry market research indicated selection as the primary criterion for customers choosing a large-format bookstore, over location, ambience, price, and service. Chapters' management focused on *selection* as its RVP for the company's large-format stores.

## SELECTION IS KEY

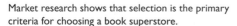
Market research shows that selection is the primary criteria for choosing a book superstore.

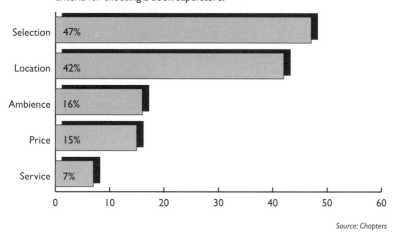

Source: *Chapters*

The focus on selection above all, within a superstore setting, paid off. Chapters was listed first in this area in the 1997 Kubas survey, and again both in 1998 and 1999. The company outpaced every other retail chain in Canada, in all product categories, including those retailers with decades of experience. The company's success was owing to the company's dedication to targeting, then creating, a strong RVP.

## CHAPTERS RATED #1 OF 130 RETAILERS

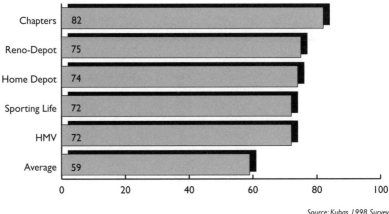

Source: Kubas 1998 Survey

Chapters' company vision of large-format, large-volume stores has distanced it from its competitors. On average, Chapters carries 105,000 titles per store, in contrast to about the 72,000 carried by its large-format bookstore competitors. Other competitors devote substantial space to candles, photo frames, and other non-book merchandise, but Chapters dedicates the bulk of its space to books. If a customer is looking for a title, the odds are that Chapters will have it. Bigger is better in this case, since more square footage obviously accommodates more shelf space, and therefore more books.

To focus on selection alone is to overlook other enablers generated by the company's large-scale operation. Larger-sized stores, selling more inventory, enabled the construction of Chapters' own distribution centre, giving the company an enviable in-stock position. In a 1998 survey by the research staff of industry publication *Quill and Quire*, 28 different books were sought in 13 bookstores. Out of these 13 stores, Chapters' four outlets in the survey finished first, second, third, and fourth in the number of titles available. No competitor outperformed *any* Chapters store. Direct fulfillment from its own distribution centre enables Chapters to pack its shelf space with more titles per shelf, and to do so more quickly. As Dennis Zook, President of Pegasus Wholesale Inc., points out, "We now ship daily to the larger volume Chapters' stores, which allows them to carry many more titles than competitors with the same shelf space."

## CHAPTERS CARRIES MORE BOOKS

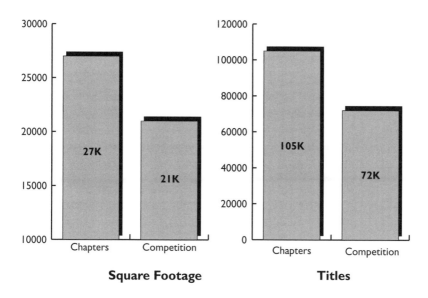

**Square Footage**          **Titles**

# *The Emotional Attraction of the Shopping Experience*

Customers have logical reasons for shopping where they do. They like the selection, the service, or the price. But there are also intangibles that direct how they choose their favourite stores – emotional reasons that account for the choices they make. Says Dan Soper, "People are attracted to fun, to stress-free shopping, to relaxation and other aspects that have nothing to do with the product for which they are shopping." Chapters has added *shopper experience* to its RVP. For example, Chapters has put enormous effort into making its children's sections both kid-proof and kid-friendly. Parents were asked to be partners in the development of the children's departments in the large stores. Their most innovative contribution was the suggestion of designing a single entrance and exit to help make it safe. Other safety mechanisms were built in as well, such as rounded corners on tables and chairs to prevent injury. A colourful decor and playful details, such as books as tall as an adult with large, turnable pages, toy trees and schoolhouses, and real aquariums encourage young

## HOW CUSTOMERS CHOOSE THEIR STORES

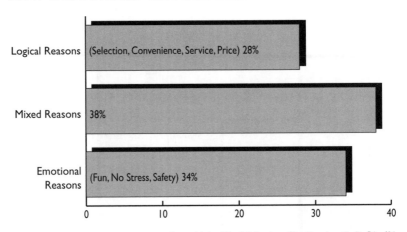

Source: National Retail Federation – "Retailing above the Rim" Jan '96

shoppers and their parents to linger, browse, and have fun. CD-ROM stations make the area interactive for today's techno-savvy kids.

For adults, a subscription to the "Active Minds" program takes participants into realms far beyond books into ones of music, academic lectures, cooking demonstrations, financial seminars, and meetings with celebrities. For example, in Toronto, a three-evening series on archaeology given by a professor from the University of Toronto provided intellectual fodder for a community gathering, while attracting faithful and prospective customers to browse the three-level downtown store. Jazz Nights held on Saturdays at the Montreal store generate a similar public response. Customers of the downtown Vancouver store brown-bag it weekly to lectures on financial topics. A presentation on space exploration at the Burlington, Ontario, store, complete with a lab setup, attracted hundreds of kids and adults.

The Chapters' RVP is well expressed in the line, "Great books are just the beginning," which is emblazoned on the entranceways to the large stores, and infused throughout the corporate culture. Books are the core of what the company represents, but the stores are designated to provide a memorable and pleasurable customer experience. They function as did the community centres of old – a place for friends to meet, to discuss ideas, listen to music, relax, browse, and, yes, buy books.

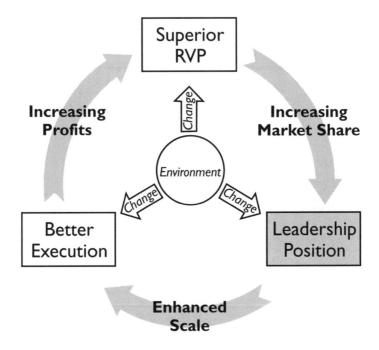

## PRINCIPLE 2:

### Achieve the leadership position in geographic markets, categories, and channels

*Chapter 4:* LEADING THE MARKET-SHARE RACE

**1.** Power retailers attain greater financial performance by achieving dominance in their selected geographic markets, product categories, and channels.

**2.** Business definition, based on degree of customer and cost sharing, determines the boundaries within which power retailers choose to compete.

# 4 Leading the Market-Share Race

*"The competition is not department stores; it's any other retailer, regardless of format, who sells our categories within our price point."*

– Paul Walters, Chairman, Sears Canada

Even with a winning RVP, retailers still fail, often because they have let competitors win the market-share race. Who hasn't witnessed the one-off shop go bankrupt, even though it appeared to offer an RVP superior to the multi-outlet competition? The second principle of retail success is that power retailers dominate their markets, playing number two to no one, and investing to outflank the current or expected future competition. Why is the pursuit of market leadership so critical, and why do so many businesses fail to achieve it?

Most retailers acknowledge the importance of achieving market leadership, but they underestimate the correlation between market share and profit. Not understanding this strong relationship contributed to the failure of several Canadian forays into the United States. Fully 90% of Canadian retailers entering the U.S. have failed – many because they neglected to apply this second principle. But Canadians are not the only ones: Marks & Spencer's announced withdrawal from the Canadian retail scene in 1999 occurred partly for the same reason: failure to build a competitive advantage through market share.

# CANADIAN RETAIL FAILURE IN THE U.S.A.

Many Canadian retailers, including some of the best in the land, like Loblaws and Canadian Tire, have failed miserably in the U.S. The Ontario Retail Sector Strategy Study highlighted that the Canadian retailer failure rate in the U.S. was almost 90%. Many factors were at work, but one of the key drivers of the dismal performance was market share. Most Canadian retailers have adopted a "toe-in-the-water" strategy because the U.S. market is so large and because a significant investment in the U.S. would put the company at risk. Unfortunately, the "toe-in-the-water" is usually bitten off when larger U.S. competitors battle the Canadian invaders. A sampling of a few of the Canadian failures in the U.S.:

**Acklands Inc.:** Purchased chain of Rose Auto Stores in 1984. Chain was placed into Chapter 11 bankruptcy in 1997 after heavy losses.

**Canadian Tire Corp.:** Bought White Stores of Wichita Falls, Texas, in 1982. Sold the auto-supply chain in 1986 after $250 million in losses. Set up Auto Source in north-central United States in 1991. Closed it in December 1994, after losses.

**Chateau Stores:** Entered U.S. in 1984 and opened more than 20 stores in the next few years. In 1991, with U.S. losses mounting, Chateau closed one-quarter of its stores. More unprofitable U.S. stores closed in 1992.

**Coles Bookstores Ltd.:** Coles opened its first store in the U.S. in 1965 in New York State and grew to 58 stores in 24 states. A minnow competing against the 1,600 mall stores operated by Waldenbooks and B. Dalton—sold its U.S. stores to Waldenbooks.

**Dylex Ltd.:** In the 1980s, bought U.S. chains Brooks Fashions, T. Edwards, Foxmoor, and others. Lost money, closed many of the stores, and Dylex slipped into creditor protection in 1995, emerging as a smaller player.

**Grafton Group Ltd.:** In 1979, acquired women's-wear chain Seifert's Inc. By 1990, Seifert's was reporting losses, and in 1992, Grafton lost control of the chains as part of a debt-reduction agreement with secured creditors in Canada.

**Imasco Ltd.:** Bought full ownership of Hardee's fast-food business in 1981. Added Roy Rogers chain in 1990. Sold both in 1997 after heavy losses.

**Loblaw:** Entered the U.S. through the acquisition of several U.S. companies beginning in 1947. U.S. operation focused on markets in New Orleans, Louisiana, and St. Louis, Missouri, and included a wholesale division. The unprofitable operation was restructured and downsized from 892 stores in 1975 to 102 stores in 1989.

**Mark's Work Wearhouse Ltd.:** Entered the U.S. in 1981 by opening two stores, eventually expanding to 10. In 1987, the U.S. operation filed for bankruptcy. Abandoned a second, more limited foray into the U.S. in the early 1990s.

**Provigo Inc.:** Entered the U.S. market in 1977 with the purchase of Market Wholesales, a Northern California food wholesaler, and Tidewater, a Chicago and New York wholesaler. In 1988, Provigo bought supermarkets in the San Franciso Bay area. By 1994, the grocery chain had left the U.S. market, selling its money-losing business in California.

**Peoples Jewellers Corp.:** Bought two big Texas-based chains, Zale in 1986 and Gordon Jewelry in 1989. Both ended up in Chapter 11 bankruptcy.

**Shoppers Drug Mart:** Entered U.S. in 1972 with its first store in Florida. The stores initially made money, but then the red ink started to flow. Sold stores to its parent company in 1984.

Add to this list a few other Canadian companies who have packed their bags and headed back north of the 49th: Black's Photography, Color Your World Inc., Consumers Distributing Inc., Cotton Ginny, Dalmy's, Laura Secord, Pennington Stores Ltd., Reitmans, Second Cup Ltd., Shirley K., St. Clair Paint & Wallpaper, and The Brick.

## Leadership Predicts Profitability – The Evidence

In retailing, leadership is necessary to be sustainably profitable. This fact is borne out in study after study and business after business. Our analysis of 226 retailers showed that this relationship holds for our power retailers, the pack, and the precarious as well. As Figure 4.1 shows, the relationship between returns and relative market share is very strong within our retail data set. RVP-superior retailers earn greater than 50% more than those retailers with average RVPs, while RVP laggards actually lose money.

### FIGURE 4.1

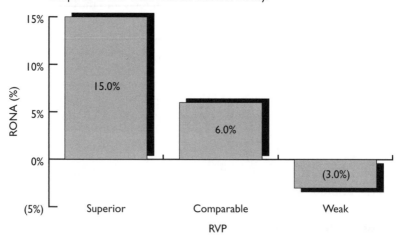

**RONA by RVP**
RVP-superior retailers earned 15% RONA,
compared to RVP-weak retailers that lost money.

Source: Canada Disclosure; Standard & Poor Stock Prices; Hoover's Online; OneSource; Annual Reports

This relationship is true for retailers as well as for other industries. Figures from the Profit Impact of Marketing Strategies (PIMS) database in the United States illustrate this point in Figure 4.2.

The PIMS data track pretax return on investment for over 3,000 businesses. Companies with relative market share under 10% average a 9% pretax return on investment. Companies that lead with more than 40% market share achieve a pretax return on

## FIGURE 4.2

### Importance of Market Share

The PIMS database demonstrates that, on average, across industries, companies with greater market share have higher profitability.

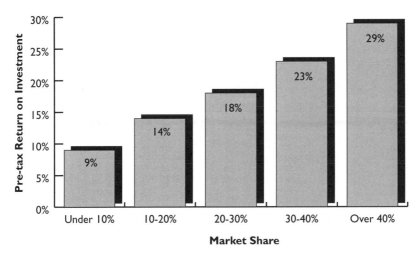

Source: PIMS (Data from 1970 to the present of 3,200 U.S. businesses)

investment of 29%. While market share alone may not entirely explain the difference in profitability, the fact remains that dominant companies across all industries earn, on average, more than three times what their lower-share competitors earn.

These data on market share need to be further refined to reflect relative, rather than absolute, market share. If two retailers in different retail sectors each have a 20% share of their markets, would we expect them to earn similar, if not identical, returns? Perhaps, but what if one of these companies had a competitor with 60% share (obviously a dominant competitor) while the other had several competitors, each with 5 to 15% of the market? In the second case, 20% was enough for clear leadership – in the first, our 20% retailer was only one-third the size of the leader. Clearly, the 20% market-share player with several small competitors, being the leader in the category, should earn far more than the former, even though each had 20% of the market.

## VIRTUAL MARKET SHARE

Market share may be even more important for virtual retailers than it has been for their bricks-and-mortar competitors. Although setting up on the Net may appear to be easy, the reality is that building a world-class site is very costly. The combination of increasing economic returns based on marginal, incremental variable costs; positive feedback loops; tremendous economies of scale and lock-in (the likelihood of keeping customers who have already developed a relationship with a site) dramatically increase the value of market share on the Internet. As Mary Meeker, Morgan Stanley's Internet analyst, likes to say, "On the Web being No. 1 is awesome, No. 2 is okay, No. 3 is tough, No. 4 is the pits, No. 8, Huh? Who?"

Additionally, virtual-market leaders trade at significant higher P/E (price-earnings ratio) multiples than their competitors. This allows these leaders to have a lower cost of capital and to be the aggregators (if money is cheaper, it is easier to invest) of their sectors as shown in the chart below.

### Virtual Market Share

| | | Market Value Multiples of 1999 E-Revenues | |
| | | Leader | Comparables Average |
| Leader | Comparables | | |
|---|---|---|---|
| Online Aggregators/Portals Yahoo! | Excite, Infoseek, Lycos GeoCities | 93.0× | 35.1× |
| Online Service Providers @HomeNetwork | America Online | 64.7× | 17.1× |
| Website Design and Services broadcast.com | Exodus, Digital Rive, USWeb | 87.4× | 11.2× |
| Internet Software Inktomi | NetGravity, Netscape RealNetworks | 45.7× | 16.2× |
| Commerce–Principal Model amazon.com | Beyond.com, Cdnow Cyberian Outpost, Egghead, Intuit, OnSale, uBid | 14.7× | 3.2× |
| Commerce–Agent Model ebay | E*Trade, Peapod, PreviewTravel | 143.5× | 8.5× |

Relative market share, not absolute share, drives profitability. Clearly, in retail as in other industries, market share – specifically relative market share – is directly correlated to profits, and without leadership share, it is difficult if not impossible to lead in the profit race.

That market share is key to successful retail strategy is hardly a new insight. The ubiquitous "cluster strategy" – placing many stores in one market — has been practised for years and is a way to achieve high local-market share. But the reasons for the importance of share leadership are not always obvious. Simply stated, the larger a retailer is, in relative terms, the more likely it will become larger still. Being number one allows a retailer to spend more than its competition in technology (for example), as the investment supports a greater number of stores, which may enable tremendous advantages in scale-driven parts of the cost structure.

## The Three Dimensions of Share Dominance

Power retailers think of leadership as more than a high-level goal. They strive to be the market leader along three dimensions:
* geography
* product category
* channel

### ◾ *Geographic Dominance*

Retailers often define the geographic market incorrectly – usually too broadly. The belief that a bigger geographic market is always better is false. A retailer laying claim to being the "biggest in the country" or the "leading national chain" cannot be assured of a sustainable defence against competition. In most categories of retail, the correct market definition is local or regional as opposed to national or global. Banks and automobile manufacturers need at least national, potentially North American or even global, markets due to the economics of their industries. Otherwise, these companies cannot achieve the economies of scale in purchasing, manufacturing, distribution, or marketing needed to be profitable. Canadian mall-based specialty stores also must often look at

## RELATIVE MARKET SHARE – DEFINING AND CALCULATING

Relative Market Share (RMS) is the comparison of one player's share to the leader's share. To calculate the leader's share, take the number of units sold by the leader and divide that figure by the number of units sold by the number-two player. If the market leader sold six billion units and the number-two company sold two billion, then the leader's relative market share is 3✕. In other words, the leader's market share is three times that of its nearest competitor.

For any player other than the leader, take the units sold by the company and divide it by the market leader's units-sold figure. In other words, the number of units sold by the leader becomes the denominator for calculating the relative market share of all other players.

For example, a retailer that had revenue of $600 million would have a relative market share of 0.1✕ when compared to the leader's $6 billion. We arrive at this figure by dividing 600 million by 6 billion. Anything over 1✕ indicates the company is the dominant player, while any figure less than 1✕ indicates a market follower.

To calculate relative market share, "units sold" is often used rather than revenue because the accumulated units of experience drive the potential for higher relative profitability. Although revenue figures are typically much easier to obtain, revenue masks the impact of what is and is not carried (for example, one player can have greater revenue because it carries a wider variety of categories, making comparisons to a more focused operator difficult). Ideally, one should calculate RMS as specifically as possible – down to the category if data are available.

Often, the data required to determine market share, let alone relative market share, are difficult to obtain. Trade groups, industry associations, or the industry press are good places to begin. Failing this, proxies – such as number of stores, square footage, or supplier purchases – can provide some measure of the various players' sizes in relation to each other.

their businesses on a national basis, but for one specific and unique reason – their landlords are national. Their landlords essentially force them to expand nationally, as they package deals across the country: to put a store in this great mall in Toronto requires taking space in other locations in Calgary or Edmonton. Retailers have essentially been prohibited from "cherry picking" specific, highly attractive real estate in focused regional markets, and instead have been forced to set up stores, some better than others, nationwide.

**AN INSIDE LOOK**

## SOBEY'S – OVERCOMING VULNERABILITY

Other market forces including competitors can lead companies to expand their markets. Sobey's, the leading grocer in the Maritimes, recognized the need to expand into additional markets as the entry of Loblaw and mass merchandisers began to create phenomenal price pressures. The increased competition in the Atlantic market, which represented 70% of Sobey's business but only 5% of Loblaw's, left Sobey's with three options.

"We could grow in an 'evergreen way' (building our own stores vs. acquiring someone else's), we could find an acquisition beyond Atlantic Canada, or we could get out," said Paul Sobey, President and CEO of Empire Company. "If we chose to expand beyond Atlantic Canada, we knew the acquisition would have to dominate a market segment to be profitable."

Sobey's dynamic response to the increased competition was to acquire The Oshawa Group in Toronto for $1.5 billion.

"In this business, size does matter. We could not have relied on just being in the Atlantic," said Sobey. "If we couldn't have completed the Oshawa deal, our returns would have come down because Loblaw could have held us at bay in a limited, local market."

Local-leadership strategies are also rare: most categories of retail necessitate expanding beyond one particular city in order to maximize profitability. Having said this, theatre owners and car dealers are two examples where local-market leadership is relevant. After all, the economics of each of these are driven solely by local-market factors, and having a second outlet in another city brings only limited advantages.

The third and most common way to think about the retail business is regionally. Most categories of retail, from apparel to food to drug stores to hardware, can be analyzed, strategized, and optimized regionally. Power retailers treat their regions as specific businesses, with a specific set of competitors, customers, and economics. Peter Luckhurst, from HMV, states it this way: "We have five specific regions, and each calls for a slight variation on our theme. Quebec is Quebec, Toronto and Ontario are urban, and the East, the Prairies, and B.C. each calls for its own specific actions, to vary the stores, alter the selection, and even change the prices."

The economics of most retail formats support this. In food retail, for example, a refrigerated distribution centre is a major investment, and while necessary to compete, a small number of stores would not make it economical to operate. So food retailers absolutely think of their businesses – their markets – on a regional basis.

The ability to measure relative market share in local markets is necessary to accurately project profitability for a food retailer. In Figure 4.3, a disguised national retailer's operations are measured at the local market level, then aggregated before the data are charted by region. The resulting chart again shows that market share drives profitability. The circle size in the figure represents the region's revenue. For this retailer, the Prairies and B.C. were the same size in revenue, but the B.C. operations earned significantly more because of a strong local market position.

**FIGURE 4.3**

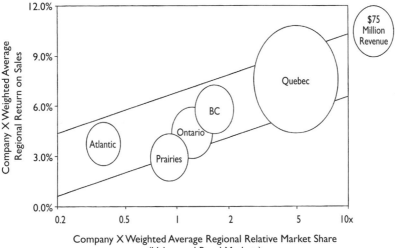

**Weighted Average Regional Market Share**

As relative market share increases, profitability (defined as Return on Sales) typically improves.

## Category Dominance

Not only is geographic leadership important; so is category leadership. In this model of retail advantage, the retailer becomes the true "category-killer" for its given product lines. In fact, Toys "R" Us is an example of both geographic and category leadership: clearly, it is the place to go for toys, but it also dominates each of its chosen geographic markets by clustering its stores in each of them. Moreover, it also measures success against every other toy retailer in its market (just as sporting goods retailer Forzani compares itself against all sporting goods retailers, including Canadian Tire and the department stores).

What power retailers have in common is that they look at competition and their businesses overall on a product-by-product, or at most a category-by-category, basis. The battle is won or lost

## AN INSIDE LOOK

### CANADIAN TIRE – DETERMINING YOUR CATEGORY

When Stephen Bachand became Chief Executive Officer of Canadian Tire in March of 1993, he took over a Canadian retailing icon. Canadian Tire had phenomenal brand awareness, a great reputation with customers, and deep financial resources. "But it was being milked," Bachand says, "We had a 'wholesaler push' mentality, and when both Wal-Mart and Home Depot came to Canada in early 1994, our stock dropped by 45%.

"One of the key things for us to get right was to decide which categories we needed to 'dominate,' versus those we had to be 'competitive' in, versus those we merely should be 'convenient' in. This analysis was done by category, by linear foot, to optimize our stores."

While Canadian Tire management knew it had to lead the automotive category (hence its May 1999 announcement to even further expand its parts business, called Auto PartSource), it could vary the offering in sporting goods.

"In tennis, we can't be dominant," Bachand explains. "It would require different services, like racquet stringing or re-gripping, and we can't do these things. But if you want your child to start in tennis, or if you need a beginner racquet yourself, we're the place. That's our tennis strategy, to be convenient, not dominant. But in fishing and camping, Canadian Tire is dominant."

against all kinds of competitors, regardless of format. These retailers know that to survive they must be the best at toys, sporting goods, or outdoor activities. Compare this to the department stores, who have largely spent the last generation thinking only in terms of format competition: as long as they were striving to be the best department store, they thought they could survive. But the harsh reality for them is that customers think of where to shop across formats, and along product lines – customers want to buy linens, not visit a department store. Customers want to buy clothing, and will go to what they consider to be the best clothing store; if this happens to be a department store, fine, if not, also fine. It is, therefore, share within a given *product category* that drives profits, not share of a given *retail format*, as shown in Figure 4.4. The department store in this example makes higher profits in women's fashion where it is dominant and makes less profit in less dominant categories.

**FIGURE 4.4**

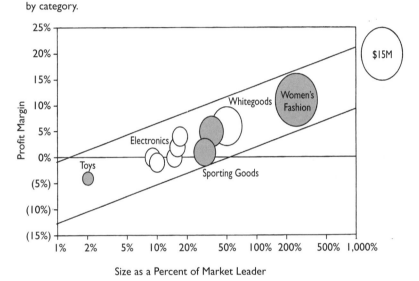

**Category Profitability/Impact of Competitive Position**
For this department store, profitability is determined by competitive position by category.

## ■ *Channel Dominance*

Increasingly, channel dominance is becoming as important as geographic and category leadership. Power retailers address the question, "Does dominance in this specific channel (route of product distribution) allow for a sustainable advantage, or is it the same business as another channel?" Amazon.com, for example, dominates the Internet channel for book retailing. The costs of Internet bookselling have to date been unique to its specific channel, so being the dominant Web-based bookseller has worked for Amazon, even if profits have been non-existent. Amazon is now moving into the distribution business, with warehouses across the U.S., just as Barnes & Noble, the number-one book retailer in the U.S., is moving into on-line selling. Suddenly, the Internet and the traditional channels are becoming one business, as more and more costs (purchasing, distribution, advertising) are actually common to both channels. Figure 4.5 illustrates this movement to one business, as Barnes & Noble, which has already brought together mall stores and superstores, enters Web-based retail.

**FIGURE 4.5**

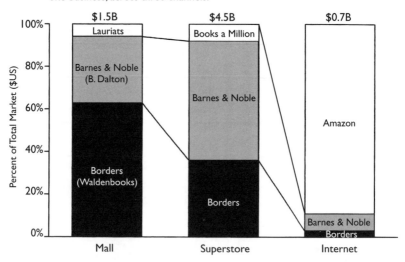

### U.S. Market Share by Channel Books

Increasingly, the U.S. book-retailing business is converging to become one business, across three channels.

*Source:* Company Financials, *Publisher's Weekly*

## ▪ *Defining the Business*

Seeking dominance on the dimensions of geography, category, or channel hinges on a proper definition of the business. Defining the business properly is as much an art as it is a science.

Cost sharing versus customer sharing is one way to define a business. High cost and high customer sharing normally indicate

## SEARS CANADA – MULTI-CHANNELS LEADS TO BRANDING

Paul Walters, Chairman of Sears Canada and the Retail Council of Canada's 1999 Retailer of the Year, lives the issue of channel leadership every day. "Our aim is to be thought of as a brand, not really as a store, and we have to know that it is profitable to sell to a customer from a whole host of channels. So whether our customer buys from us in our catalogue, store, or Internet site doesn't really matter."

This perspective has driven Sears to change its entire organization. Says Walters, "We are no longer organized in silos – like IT, retail stores, etc. – but are today arranged by business, like furniture or hardware, that cuts across all channels. We need consistency channel to channel and this way we get it much more easily.

"The store is a dated concept. It is nothing more than a place where you transact business. The customer is much more important, and you will have to use a host of different channels to give the customer what she wants."

one business. For example, charge cards and credit cards are the same business – the reason for this is that there is significant customer overlap and a high degree of shared cost. But in retail, who would have predicted that Petro-Canada would be in the same business as Becker's? By looking at customers, one could have seen that convenience is key to both retailers' customers, and that gas stations looking to leverage their fixed costs (rent and labour) would move into convenience-store retailing. High customer sharing implies that the same customer on the same trip makes purchases with the same criteria.

On the other hand, low cost sharing and low customer sharing would point toward two separate businesses. The movie theatre business and food stores, for example, are clearly separate businesses, as the economies of the two are completely different from each other and there is virtually no customer sharing.

## SEPHORA – TAKING AIM AT DEPARTMENT STORES

Sephora, a chain of 239 stores in Europe and the U.S., is a retailer that is taking dead aim at category leadership. Sephora's concept is to be the world's first cosmetics category-killer (a retailer that achieves dominance in its category), selling 13,000 items in its stores, with products merchandised not by brand but by product category. This merchandising approach makes comparison shopping much easier.

Unlike department stores, where cosmetics are arranged by brand and salespeople are essentially commissioned sales representatives of these cosmetics companies, Sephora pays no commissions, offers no free gifts, and its prices are neither higher nor lower than major competitors'.

Sephora has added unique concepts to the cosmetics business, including interactive kiosks that provide information and customer advice based on the customer's profile. Customers have reacted positively to Sephora's elegant store design and decor.

Unfortunately for department stores, this category-killer concept (which requires stores in the 20,000-square-foot range) will hit them where they are most vulnerable: many department stores earn up to 20% of their profits from cosmetics. And Sephora has very aggressive growth plans – it expects to go from 18 to 51 stores in the U.S. by its year-end in 1999 – and deep pockets, as it is owned by LVMH Moët Hennessy Louis Vuitton.

Sephora is but the latest to prove the evolving cross-format, category-specific nature of retail. It happened in toys, appliances and electronics years earlier.

By looking at retail categories on a two-by-two matrix, as shown in Figure 4.6 (customer sharing versus cost/economics sharing), one can correctly determine the boundaries of a given business. The questions of who are the relevant competitors, how to grow into related categories, or who may become a competitor can all be addressed through this analytic tool.

**FIGURE 4.6**

### Defining the Business

Cost sharing and customer sharing are the primary determinants of
business definition, and highlight the business boundaries.

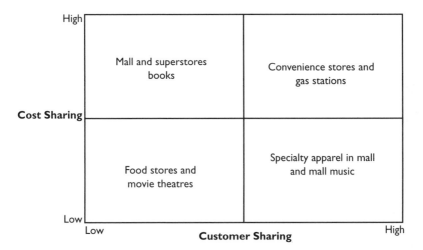

## Summary

Power retailers focus on dominating the markets they choose
to compete in. Successful retailers make sure of one thing: that
in their chosen geographic market, category, or channel, they
will be the player all other retailers monitor and react to. They
understand precisely the economics of their business and define
their business based on realistic, data-driven assessments of their
markets.

# Leadership—Driver of Financial Performance

Chapters believes that market leadership is an important driver of financial performance. The logic of the 1995 merger was that uniting two relatively financially unattractive businesses, SmithBooks and Coles, would result in one strong cash-generative company – one that would provide the funds needed to invest in a new breed of larger stores. But generating a strong market leader and a cash-generative business first was imperative. Only then could the new growth concept of superstores be developed.

Chapters strives to be the market leader by both category and geographic market. In the mall stores, the choice was made to purposefully build upon the company's category dominance in the selling of books and other related items, and to minimize or eliminate altogether the peripheral videos, toys, and stationery supplies. Observes Harry Yanowitz, "We found out which products were profitable, and which products suffered from a weak competitive position."

Leaving the bottom three product areas behind, Chapters focused on the upper group, which considerably improved overall profitability in the mall stores. As Sarah Strachan, Senior Vice-President, Mall Stores, says, "As a result of focus, we did a much better job on books and magazines instead of splitting our efforts."

Market share by product and profitability were clearly correlated. The highest profit was provided by proprietary publishing – specifically Coles Notes and other books the company produced itself. As Nigel Berrisford, Vice-President of Publishing, says, "Since we are the only outlet for some of these volumes, we can achieve very respectable profit margins." Next in line was the much wider category of books in general, which had a much higher volume of sales, and in which Chapters was now the market leader.

Other companies had already established market leadership in the three product categories at the bottom of the list – stationery, videos, and toys. In stationery it was Grand and Toy, and Business Depot; in videos,

**Mall Bookstore Profitability By Product**

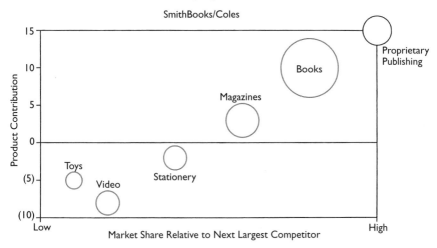

Relative importance in market share per product is indicated by the circles in the above chart.

Blockbuster and Rogers; and in toys, Toys "R" Us, Wal-Mart, and a host of competitors. The company had very little market share in these three categories and was losing money. Realizing it couldn't compete in these product areas, Chapters stopped selling all three products in its mall stores. The company took massive markdowns, had blowout sales on videos, closed its eight acquired toy stores, and ended the back-to-school loss-leader stationery sales that Coles had been accustomed to running in the fall of every year.

Chapters believes that market share is important in product terms, but also important in geographic markets, which are generally defined locally for book retailers. As shown in the chart on page 110, strong market-share regions for Chapters did well financially, while weaker competitive markets fared worse financially.

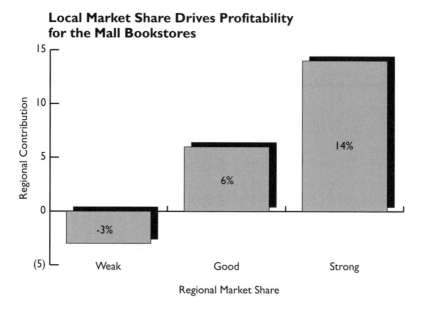

**Local Market Share Drives Profitability
for the Mall Bookstores**

Chapters also set out to achieve *geographic leadership,* to be the largest book retailer across the country, market by market, and mapped out the top 25 Canadian markets with high university-graduate populations. Then, city by city, province by province, Chapters opened more outlets than all the competition combined from coast to coast.

Market share has enormous implications for successful retailing, on both the local and national levels. At the local level, clustering stores in one area creates benefits in at least four main facets of company operations:

- store operations
- customer convenience
- share of mind
- advertising

## *1. Store Operations*
Having a cluster of stores in one area affords the possibility of engaging a senior-level district manager who can ensure that the stores are being well managed and operating at optimum levels. The critical mass also allows

for a level of training that is not possible for a single store. Dan Soper, Senior VP of Large-Format Operations, asserts that, "We upgrade our operational performance significantly when we can have multiple stores in one market." National market share then builds upon local market leadership, and creates a new range of benefits. By 1999, Chapters had built a $570 million business, enabling it to invest more than $10 million into its own national shipping centre, which services its stores from coast to coast, as well as Internet orders.

## 2. Customer Convenience

Senior VP of Marketing and Merchandising David Hainline points out, "Our loyalty members appreciate the benefits of shopping in five or six of our stores in one market area, so that they can get discounts near home or work, or close to their friends."

## 3. Share of Mind

The more stores in a local market, the more the public is aware of them. A multitude of similar storefronts, with their familiar logos and company identities, have the same impact as repeat advertising.

## 4. Advertising

Market dominance inevitably increases advertising scale while dramatically reducing costs, and allows a common voice for multiple stores. In a market with five or six stores, such as in Calgary, Chapters can capitalize on a single ad in the local paper for all of its stores. As David Hainline says, "This effectively gives us much more share of book advertising at a fraction of the per-store cost, compared to a competitor with only one or two stores." A blanket ad in Calgary, Ottawa, or Toronto spreads the promotional dollar value among several stores.

## Competing in Three Channels

Chapters is really three separate but highly related businesses: the mall stores, the large-format Chapters stores, and the Internet. While there is overlap in service, customers of each business are regarded as distinct from each other. Customer sharing occurs, but in specific ways: mall stores with the Internet, and large-format stores with the Internet. There is little customer sharing between large-format and mall stores. The latter tend to be distinct customers with distinct needs (convenience rather than selection).

The geographic definition of each business is unique. The large-format business is first and foremost local. Thus, a superstore operator can be very successful and have only three outlets in one market, since they would be leveraging operational scale at a local level. Chapters, while researching its own prospective approach, found that many U.S. players had proved successful in a single market. The Tattered Cover in Denver, for example, had locations only in the one city, but achieved tremendous market and mind share. In Miami, book lovers might not have a clue what The Tattered Cover was, but it is a moot point.

In contrast to the large-format stores, the mall business is primarily regional, though it has a national aspect: nationwide stores naturally encourage relationships with national landlords, such as Cadillac-Fairview, Cambridge, or Oxford. A company can be very successful at operating only 10 or 15 bookstores in one city, but a national presence is required to acquire access into many of the prime malls.

The Internet business is a national business. Given the scale of the Canadian Internet market, and the costs and investment needed to be a world class e-commerce site, it isn't possible to be just a regional player. The Internet shares many of the front-end costs with the large Chapters stores, such as brand-building and customer relationships.

All three businesses share money costs at the back end (e.g., finance, systems and construction), and this serves to improve Chapters' cost position and, hence, profit performance. Most importantly, all businesses share fulfillment, which gives Chapters sales and cost advantages over its competitors. Chapters' approach to bookselling ensures that it is the market leader by product, geography, and channel.

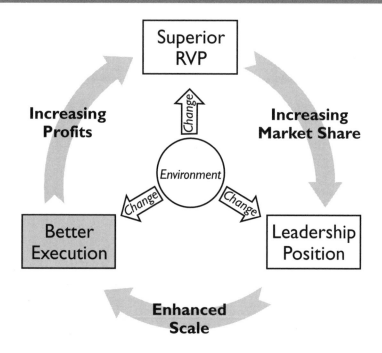

# Execute better than competitors in the areas of people, technology and costs

***Chapter 5:*** INVESTING IN PEOPLE TO ACHIEVE CUSTOMER LOYALTY
1. There is a clear link between employee commitment and customer loyalty. Power retailers achieve customer loyalty by investing in their people.
2. They invest by hiring the right people, enabling them, and by motivating their staff through superior leadership, compensation, and constant celebration
3. Power retailers measure their return on people investment through objective feedback loops. This feedback guides continuous improvement.

***Chapter 6:*** MANAGING INFORMATION TECHNOLOGY FOR STRATEGIC BREAKTHROUGHS
1. Power retailers use information technology to manage merchandise selection and store planning.
2. They also customize their marketing using customer database management and innovative loyalty programs.
3. Information technology enables strategic breakthroughs such as Internet retailing.

***Chapter 7:*** COST MANAGEMENT TO MINIMIZE MARGIN EROSION
1. Managing costs is critical to maintaining sustainable advantage in a thin-margin business like retail. Power retailers focus on managing the key cost areas that most affect profits.
2. Power retailers manage and optimize their product category portfolio to maximize returns.
3. They share experience internally to continually improve, and also consider the entire value chain to look for economies beyond their business borders.

# 5 Investing in People to Achieve Customer Loyalty

> *"We want to differentiate our employment experience. How a company behaves internally determines how it behaves externally; if we listen to our store managers, they will listen to our customers."*
>
> – Peter Luckhurst, President of HMV U.S. and Canada

Achieving dominant market share, as discussed in the previous chapter, lays the foundation for strong financial performance. As seen in Figure 5.1, the improvement in relative market share generally will drive performance up and to the right on the chart, leading to superior returns. But improved strategic position establishes only the *potential* for improved financial returns. Achieving this potential is completely dependent on a successful execution of the retailer's strategy.

The first two principles – (1) deliver a customer-driven, superior RVP and (2) achieve leading market position in geographic market, category, and channel – were about *doing the right things*. This third principle of retailing is about *doing things right*: Executing better than competitors in the areas of people, cost, and technology.

In our survey, retail CEOs were virtually unanimous in their opinion that the power retailers are separated from the pack

**FIGURE 5.1**

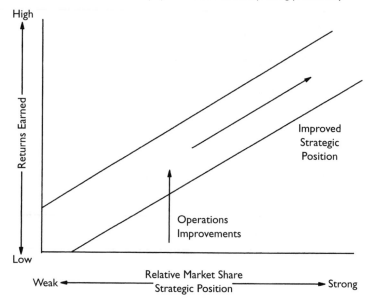

**Performance Improvement**
While strategic excellence leads to sustainably improved performance,
excellence in execution plays a critical role in improving profitability.

thanks to superior execution. As Clare Copeland, the former CEO
of Peoples Jewellers, claims, "So much of retail is execution which
is basically discipline." Superior execution is a broad statement
and clearly encompasses hundreds of imperatives. As Canadian
Business Hall of Famer Jean Coutu recently said in his acceptance
speech, "Take care of the details and the rest will follow." Our survey of retail CEOs pinpointed the key areas of focus for successful
retail execution, shown here in Figure 5.2.

The next three chapters will cover three critical components
of execution which together comprise our third principle for
successful retailers: execute through people (this chapter), costs
(Chapter 6) and technology (Chapter 7). Chapter 7 will encom-
pass the topic of customer retention and loyalty programs, which
are enabled by a sophisticated IT strategy.

**FIGURE 5.2**

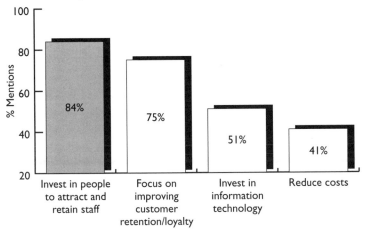

### The Key Elements of Retail Execution

*Source: 1998 Retail CEO Survey*

As seen in Figure 5.2, our retail CEOs strongly believe that people are the most important element in any retailer's ability to successfully execute a strategy day in and day out. Creating the superior retail value proposition is the first step to greater profits, but ultimately it is the retailer's staff who must deliver the RVP. Essentially, the winning retailers know that when they treat staff well, staff will treat customers well. Satisfied employees generate greater customer satisfaction, which in turn leads to increased customer loyalty. As a point of differentiation, the power retailers invest in their people.

The correlation between satisfied staff and business success is even higher in retail because employees are truly the retailers' only sustainable asset. Despite the importance of people to retail success, most retail employees do not like their jobs. A U.S. survey of 1,400 retail management and front-line employees by Terri Kabachnic Company Inc. showed that a whopping 73% "hate" their jobs. Part of the reason for this dismal performance is that managing people in retail presents several organizational challenges, because of the nature of the typical retail work world:

- *First job:* For many retail employees, this is their first job. Having never worked before, they often have unrealistic expectations of what working life is like. Many retailers fail to meet these expectations.
- *Low Pay:* Generally, retail employees receive lower wages than employees in other industry sectors. This low pay often leads to underinvestment by retailers in hiring quality staff and in lower ongoing investment once the employee is onboard.
- *High Turnover:* Low pay means that retail is often just a way station for staff and not a planned career. High turnover means that retailers often invest too little in training. This underinvestment and low pay lead to high turnover.
- *Part-time:* Many retail workers are part-time, which makes communication and training difficult for the retailer and makes career commitment impossible for the employee who cannot sustain a living on part-time hours.
- *Geographic dispersion:* For the national scale retailer, employees are dispersed across the country. This makes communication, which is vital to job satisfaction, more difficult.

*Power retailers understand that their people are the most important factor in their ability to successfully execute a winning strategy day in and day out.*

Power retailers understand they must develop means to address these issues for their staff. Generally they pay better than their competitors, have lower turnover rates, make extra efforts to communicate effectively despite the constraints of time and geography, and are outstanding at setting realistic expectations about the demands of the retail environment for potential staff.

Power retailers understand that winning with customers means first of all winning with employees. Southwest Airlines'

## CIBC – COMPETING THROUGH PEOPLE

**AN INSIDE LOOK**

In Canada's increasingly competitive financial services world, the winning banks are outpacing the competition with a renewed focus on increasing the loyalty of their best customers. In this endeavour, CIBC is taking a lead in research and implementation strategies.

CIBC wants its customers to not only buy all of their financial products from CIBC, but also wants to increase customer loyalty so that these customers will recommend CIBC to their friends. Getting this intense customer loyalty starts with employee commitment.

Senior Vice-President Adrian Horwood states that strategically CIBC is attuned to the "strong and very direct linkages between employment commitment and customer loyalty."

CIBC's initial research of this critical link was designed to "get empirical data on the impact various employee initiatives are having on employee commitment, customer loyalty, and our financial performance," explains Don McCreesh, former Executive Vice-President, Human Resources, at CIBC. In banking, a high percentage of employees have direct customer dealings. Notably, the research showed that the factors that drive employee satisfaction differ across the business units, with customer service orientation being a top driver.

In comparing its statistical data at the district level, CIBC determined that a 5% improvement in employee commitment increases customer loyalty by 2%, which in turn improves profitability by 2%. Branches with the highest levels of employee commitment also show the highest levels of customer loyalty.

**Behaviours Generate Value**

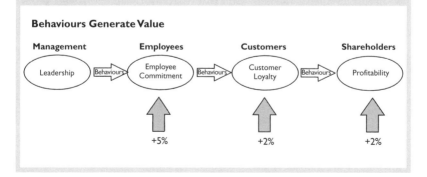

What factors influence employee commitment at CIBC? As part of its research, CIBC conducted open forums at district and branch levels to encourage employee feedback, and also carried out annual employee surveys and follow-up focus groups. CIBC identified the factors that had the greatest impact on employee commitment and satisfaction – culture, leadership, customer service, workload, learning opportunities, and rewards and recognition. By empowering its teams to act on their own suggestions and ideas, CIBC is creating a positive employee experience that produces greater customer loyalty and better business results.

Don McCreesh likens the end result to a "virtuous circle." Employees enjoy working for a customer-focused organization and that, in turn, creates satisfied, loyal customers and a stronger business. As he says, "It becomes mutually reinforcing."

legendary CEO Herb Kelleher claims that customers are only his number-two priority, his employees are his number-one priority. If he takes care of his number-one priority, they will take care of his number-two priority. This attitude has led to both outstanding staff relations and unparalleled customer service relative to other airlines.

FIGURE 5.3

## The Employee Customer Profit Chain at Sears

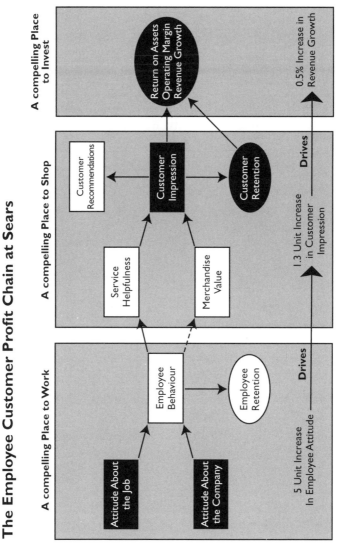

Source: *Harvard Business Review, January–February 1998*

Arthur Martinez, Sears' CEO, and his senior managers developed a business model that tracked the company's success from management behaviour to employee attitudes to customer satisfaction and financial performance. Today, Sears' model, as shown in Figure 5.3, serves as a key part of its management information and decision-making process.

Sears wanted to build a company that was "a compelling place to work, a compelling place to shop and a compelling place to invest." Management believed that achieving these three goals would satisfy and energize employees, customers, and investors.

Sears' statistical analysis showed that a 5-unit increase in employee attitude drove a 1.3-unit increase in customer impression, which in turn led to a 0.5% increase in revenue growth. Thus a store that could improve by 5 points on the employee survey side could expect to gain an additional 0.5% in revenue growth. The key was to ensure that its employees were satisfied and committed. These employees, in turn, would ensure that customers loved to shop at Sears.

And the impact of these insights on Sears' strategy? According to an article in the January–February 1998 *Harvard Business Review*, Sears increased employee satisfaction by 4% and in turn customer satisfaction by the same 4% in one year alone. These increases generated an additional $200 million in revenue for Sears over that same year. And it doesn't end there. Using the business model it developed in the initial research and analysis, Sears continues to focus on the process of constant improvement. Now every year, Sears recalculates the connection between management behaviour, employee attitudes, customer satisfaction, and financial performance to stay abreast of the changing economy, changing demographics, and changing competitive environment. As Sears Canada Chairman and CEO Paul Walters says, "You can't grow by 25% without more and happier customers, and we think there's a definite link between employee satisfaction and customer satisfaction. You can't have cranky employees and happy customers!"

## AN INSIDE LOOK

## SEARS – DEFINITION OF A "COMPELLING PLACE TO WORK"

In analyzing employees' responses to a 70-question survey, Sears observed that its employees' rating on ten key questions, designed to elicit attitudes about the job and the company, produced the highest indicators of employee behaviour:

1. I like the kind of work I do.
2. My work gives me a sense of accomplishment.
3. I am proud to say I work at Sears.
4. How does the amount of work you are expected to do influence your overall attitude about your job?
5. How do your physical working conditions influence your *overall attitude* about your job?
6. How does the way you are treated by those who supervise you influence your *overall attitude* about the job?
7. I feel good about the future of the company.
8. Sears is making the changes necessary to compete effectively.
9. I understand our business strategy.
10. I see a connection between the work I do and the company's strategic objectives.

As discussed in the January–February 1998 *Harvard Business Review*, Sears found that "two dimensions of employee satisfaction – attitude toward the job and toward the company – had a greater effect on employee loyalty and behaviour towards customers than all the other dimensions put together." While they still use the 70-question survey to gather information about working conditions and satisfaction with pay and benefits, Sears views the ten questions above as a "report card on management" that clearly relates management skills to the achievement of company goals.

## Successfully Investing in People – Three Key Steps

Clearly there is a correlation between financial performance and a retailer's ability to lead its people well. Based on our analysis of the power retailers, we believe there are three key steps to developing the right "people strategy" and to achieving a high "return on people investment":

1. Hire the right people.
2. Enable staff by empowering, communicating, and training.
3. Motivate people and align them with the strategy through leadership, compensation, and constant celebration.

### ■ 1. Hire the Right People

Given the correlation between satisfied employees and strong fiscal performance, one of the keys to investing wisely in the organization's people is to hire the right people in the first place. Of course, the retailer needs to be able to identify who the right people are.

Companies like Peoples Jewellers understand that the right people to bring onboard are those very similar to people already achieving success within the current organization. Peoples and other power retailers focus on identifying the common traits of people who have had success in their organizations. The strategy then becomes to recruit more of the same – people who exhibit the proven attributes for success in their company. Pushed to an extreme, however, this leads to a very homogeneous organization. Diversity *is* needed too. As Tom Wolfe, former CEO of Bombay Company Canada, and CEO of The Bentley Agnew Group, states, "We need diverse people in an organization so that we remain entrepreneurial, so that you can continue to reinvent. Without diverse people, no one disagrees with me."

These retailers are also able to identify those who are simply seeking work and have no intention of staying. Without a clear perception of the right people, the retailer soon learns that in spite of a substantial investment in training, some employees soon leave to pursue other aspirations. These are the recruits that view the job as a way station until something better comes along. While the retailer will always have turnover, a focused selection strategy can reduce the likelihood of hiring job-sitters.

*The power retailers identify the common traits of people who have had success in their organization and then try to recruit more of the same.*

Au Bon Pain, the U.S. food service company, invests significantly more than most retailers in hiring the right people. As Len Schlesinger, who served as Au Bon Pain's Chief Operating Officer, observed in "Breaking the Cycle of Failure in Service" in the *Sloan Management Review*: "An integral part of the Au Bon Pain selection process is a paid two-day work experience in the store prior to final selection interviews. This experience weeds out applicants both through self-selection and management observation of behaviour."

Of course, getting the right people requires attracting the right applicants in the first place. The winning retailers dominate both market share and worker share. They are the preferred places to work. And once so established, the retailers then attract many more of these talented "right" people to apply for the jobs.

## 2. Enable Staff

Once the retailer has succeeded in getting the right people to apply for the job, the next step is convincing them to stay. In focusing on staff retention, the power retailers invest massive amounts of time and money and involve senior management.

Enabling people to do their jobs involves empowering, communicating, and training. Empowering is probably one of the most overused management terms of the decade but it is one of the key attributes of successful retailers. As Peter Luckhurst of HMV states, "We are genuine about our store managers being autonomous, but it is not anarchy or laissez-faire. We want our store managers to feel ownership, but there are strong control systems." The key is to give front-line employees the power and authority to help their customers. Ritz-Carlton is legendary in this domain since they allow any employee to do whatever it takes to rectify a guest's complaint or problem, on the spot, up to a total cost of $2,000.

On a recent trip to the Grand Floridian Hotel in Disney World, a guest asked a gardener on the grounds if he could help her with a squeaking wheel on her stroller. Clearly this was not in his job description. He dropped everything and miraculously reappeared five minutes later with WD40 and fixed the problem. She thanked him profusely and he proudly asked if she knew what the "Grand" in Grand Floridian stood for. He recited that "**G**uest **R**equests **A**re **N**ever **D**enied." Disney has done a wonderful job of empowering their staff to solve customer issues.

*Front-line employees need the power and authority to help their customers, and to understand not only how their store is performing but how products and various placements within the store affect profitability.*

A large part of Disney's success in empowering and enabling employees is the fact that they invest heavily in communication to their staff. As Clare Copeland of Peoples states, "A lot has to do with communication. We must make sure that the fog index is low, that the communication is clear." Balancing employee empowerment and accountability requires sharing as much information as is possible so that employees can make the right decisions for doing their jobs appropriately and correctly. For retailers, this information is primarily financial. Employees need to understand not only how their store performs but also how products and even the various placements within the store affect profitability. It also means communicating those things that are important to the employees. This latter communication requires management to hone its listening skills as well as provide opportunities for employees to share their thoughts.

The champion retailers demonstrate many different approaches to encouraging employee feedback – for example, setting up

## AN INSIDE LOOK

### LONDON DRUGS – BUILDING A FAMILY

The Louie family firm has built one of Canada's most successful retail chains in the drug store sector. Dominating its chosen markets in the provinces of British Columbia and Alberta, London Drugs is reputed to have the highest sales per square foot of any drug store chain in North America. What does it consider to be the backbone of its success? Its employees.

Like most power retailers, London Drugs has a strong and definable culture. Its employees work very hard and are very competitive. Most of all, they love to work in a team-based environment that allows tremendous latitude. At the end of a store manager's meeting when these enthusiastic employees belt out the song "We Are Family," they mean it.

When asked to describe the key to their job satisfaction, most employees say trust is the word that first comes to mind – obviously an essential requirement for any retailer with pharmacy as its core and a key value proposition for its customers.

To ensure that it attracts and selects the right people for the organization, London Drugs has chosen a growth strategy that is cautious compared to the rapid expansion of some of the champion retailers. It adds only three to four stores a year and now stands at 48 stores. This carefully structured growth gives the management team, led by President and COO Wynne Powell, sufficient time to ensure new employees understand and embrace the values of London Drugs. It also means that job applicants are numerous for the few highly sought positions in this successful retail chain.

hotlines to a support office with 1-800 numbers or completing climate surveys either on a sample basis or coast to coast. Some provide upward feedback forms to allow staff to say what they think of their direct supervisors (which is often a true reflection of what these employees think of the entire company). Others hold meetings, either on an ad hoc or formal basis, to get valuable information from their employees, especially on what needs to be changed. And when employees leave, these retailers conduct exit interviews to discuss their decision.

# MOUNTAIN EQUIPMENT CO-OP – COMMITMENT TO THE ENVIRONMENT AND THEIR EMPLOYEES

Known as a store for grown-ups who love wilderness recreation, Mountain Equipment Co-op offers a fabulous selection of outdoor equipment for outdoor enthusiasts at all levels of ability. But what differentiates it from its competitors is its floor staff. As CEO Bill Gibson says, "Mountain Equipment Co-op wants to be the best place to work and the best place to shop in Canada – we need to be both."

A not-for-profit co-operative, Mountain Equipment is committed to supporting many worthwhile environmental, education and advocacy causes through its Environment Fund and its Endowment Fund for the Environment. This demonstrated care for the community-at-large makes its staff proud to work there and be part of the sustainability efforts.

Not only are staff proud to be part of the MEC team, but they enjoy coming to work every day. The organization has initiated many unique benefit programs that strengthen job satisfaction and loyalty. These programs also ensure that staff have tremendous knowledge about MEC's products and activities and can effectively serve MEC members.

To foster product knowledge and hands-on experience, MEC offers staff equipment purchases and loans at minimal cost. Extremely flexible working arrangements let those who would prefer to be trekking the Himalayas apply for a leave of absence to follow their dreams. Recently, a store manager left for three months to climb K2. For members, these incentives mean that mountain-climbing enthusiasts can discuss pitons with someone who has actually climbed or kayaks with someone who has actually paddled on the Ottawa River.

In addition, buyers take time to discuss the features and benefits of new products with store staff. For the type of employee attracted to work there, these in-store seminars also enhance their enjoyment of their recreational pursuits. Every store recently had about 25 of its staff members to a two-hour early-morning presentation on sleeping bags.

Mountain Co-op invests heavily in training. In fact, new recruits do not even deal with members until after they complete an introductory 10-day training program. To encourage continuous training, employees receive merit pay bonuses when they pass certain product training modules such as "Backpacking 1."

Compensation is also an important factor in attracting and retaining staff. Mountain Equipment Co-op pays well above average wages for floor staff and offers a generous leave of 12 "care days" per year for illness or family crises such as a funeral. Its Prosperity Sharing program lets employees share in the profits – each can earn up to an extra 2% twice a year.

And in addition to the benefits, training, and financial incentives they receive, employees know their opinions are listened to and acted upon. Twice a year, Bill visits each store to sit in the "hot seat" to listen and respond to staff's concerns and ideas.

In all, Mountain Equipment Co-op's commitment to its employees fosters a positive attitude. In turn, its employees' enthusiasm translates into increased member satisfaction and Mountain Equipment Co-op's dominant market position.

Staff who know what is going on and expected of them, and are empowered to do their job, still need one last critical ingredient to be fully enabled – the skill to excel in their roles. Power retailers train their employees for success.

Training includes explaining company expectations, norms, and values as well as ensuring candidates have an accurate description of the jobs they are being hired to do. Retail is an industry that can inspire romantic notions about working with the public. In the book-selling sector, for example, some would-be booksellers view a floor position as being a relatively fun job, one where there's an opportunity to read voraciously between chats with literary customers. However, the reality is that the job is strenuous and demanding. Employees lug boxes of books and are constantly on their feet with very little time in the store itself to be reading books. Providing honest descriptions of the job ensures that new hires have a clear understanding of the work they are expected to do.

Training is not a one-time investment for new members of the team. Organizations such as Starbucks not only invest heavily in upfront training to ensure all staff have the required skills to provide a premium level of service to its customers, but they also invest in continuous training. Refresher training is carried out every 18 to 24 months to help employees relearn basic and complementary skills so they can do their jobs even better. Retraining staff on a periodic basis also allows an organization to keep its employees abreast of changes in the marketplace so that everyone is prepared to respond to customers' new and different demands with the right product or service at the right time.

## ■ 3. Motivate and Align Staff

Power retailers motivate and align their staff with their overall strategy through strong leadership and appropriate and innovative compensation and by constantly celebrating accomplishments.

The first step is leadership. Leadership defines the vision, culture, and values of the organization. Best-selling business author Peter Drucker says, "The differences between managing a chain of retail stores and managing a Roman Catholic diocese are amazingly fewer than either retail executives or bishops realize." Given far-flung operations, both need to rely on strong cultures, values, and vision to ensure that the many disparate parts of the organizations are heading in the right direction. As Clare Copeland of Peoples comments, "When you have far and distant stores, they have to have strong leadership. In retail winners, there is clearly a leader who is in charge." But one leader cannot do it alone. Retail winners develop hundreds of leaders throughout their organization and have a strong and deep bench. As Harvard leadership professor John Kotter points out, "We are long past the time when leaders can do it all alone, or even by the dozen. It takes hundreds to lead."

*Leadership defines the vision, culture, and values of the organization. Retail winners develop hundreds of leaders throughout their organization and have a strong and deep bench.*

## HMV – CORE VALUES

Most power retailers explicitly communicate their values. As the following statement from HMV illustrates:

HMV is committed to providing a great work environment and satisfying jobs for all our employees. The following core values outline the way we believe our staff and customers should be treated:

- People are mature adults and deserve dignity.
- People want to work hard and obtain substantial fulfillment from their work.
- People want to be committed to the company and achieve personal fulfillment from this commitment.
- Performance achievement goals should always be a stretch – but they should never be unachievable.
- People can and should be trusted.
- People perform better if they have:
  - voice, a say in what affects their work
  - autonomy, the ability to contribute and add value
  - understanding, of the company's vision and values and objectives
  - security/reward: commitment is two-way
  - development: develop and utilize their skills
- People want to belong to a high-performance company.

Power retailers align their incentives with the strategy that the leadership has articulated. Incentives include promotions, recognition, and critically, compensation. People do care about their compensation and will often tailor their focus to maximize their own pay. Thus getting the incentives aligned with the strategy, direction, and values of the company is critical to the organization's success.

Most of the champion retailers provide compensation that is at least as good or better than the industry average for their sector. Nordstrom pays its salespeople on the floor 20 to 50% more than other department stores pay. Similarly, Chick-Fil-A, a $650

**AN INSIDE LOOK**

## STARBUCKS – MASTERING PEOPLE LEADERSHIP

Now the largest coffee retailer in North America, Starbucks is a master in people leadership. During its explosive growth during the 1990s, its staffing – attracting, training, motivating, and retaining the right staff – was a critical part of its successful strategy. As CEO Howard Schultz explains, "Our only sustainable competitive advantage is the quality of our people and our relationship with them."

Starbucks invests heavily in training its staff members known as "Baristas" and unlike most retailers includes part-time staff in its benefits program. It also offers employees an innovative stock plan. Called Bean Stock, the plan has a five-year vesting period. To help employees take advantage of this opportunity and to instil the team spirit, they are given grants that are tied to the company's profitability.

Overall, Starbucks' innovative compensation plan contributes to the employees' pride of ownership – and an employee turnover rate that is less than half of the industry average.

million U.S. fast food operator, also pays significantly more than its competitors in food service.

What is most interesting is not just that these retailers pay more but that the compensation is highly variable and tied to individual or team performance – after all, it is the team at store level that has to succeed, but that team also controls the elements that will make it succeed. These retailers also make the incentives simple and predictable. If it takes a team over forty-five minutes to work out what it thinks its bonus or compensation will be, the compensation scheme is probably too complex. More importantly, a scheme this complex will not motivate employees.

Many progressive retailers provide their employees with stock ownership plans or stock options so that they can share in the value that they are creating for the owners of the company. Starbucks does it through Bean Stock; Wal-Mart has created huge

**AN INSIDE LOOK**

## CHICK-FIL-A – TREATING MANAGERS LIKE OWNERS

With more than 40,000 employees, Chick-Fil-A is one of the world's best quick-service restaurant chains. And it has been in business for 52 years, all of them profitable. Its strategy? It selects the right managers and makes each feel like an owner.

Its unique incentive program requires every new store manager to invest in the store itself. As part owner, the manager shares 50% of the profits of that store. As a result, store managers make significantly more than managers of other food operations.

How do they find the right store manager? The screening process includes a 10-page questionnaire, interviews of both the applicant and his or her spouse, and an in-store internship for several days, with pay. Those who succeed in this selection process must then provide a deposit of $5,000 (which is returned if they subsequently leave). Managers are guaranteed a minimum annual income of $30,000. After paying the Atlanta head office an operating fee of 15% to cover equipment rental and administrative and support service expenses, the manager and Chick-Fil-A then split the remaining profits 50/50. The average Chick-Fil-A manager earns $45,000 compared to an industry average of $30–35,000. The top 10% of Chick-Fil-A managers earn more than $100,000.

The success of Chick-Fil-A's unique compensation scheme is now so well known that it recently attracted over 9,000 applicants for management positions at 80 new store operations.

nest eggs for many of its floor staff thanks to employee stock ownership. Providing stock as an incentive helps align incentives and also helps lower employee turnover. Home Depot's turnover amongst employees who have stock is only one-fourth of the turnover of staff who do not hold Home Depot stock.

The last, and by far the most important, aspect of compensation for all of the successful retailers exemplified by Nordstrom is that it is based on merit. Good people can do very, very well. And those people who are not very good do not have to be asked to leave. They choose to leave because their compensation does not increase at a fast enough rate.

The final piece of the motivation-and-alignment puzzle is the need to celebrate often. Great retailers find ways to keep their people pumped. Like any great sports team, champion retailers need to pause to collect the trophies and congratulate themselves on their success. Peoples Jewellers increased dramatically the number of contests and awards for sales associates and managers. Wal-Mart constantly celebrates the achievement of store and company goals. But as Dave Ferguson, CEO of Wal-Mart Canada, says, "We celebrate our achievements but then we raise the bar and we get right back to work."

Power retailers who have mastered this principle of retail success have incorporated and keep close tabs on at least three feedback loops (a concept explored further in Chapter 8) in their people management process.

1. Employee application to acceptance ratios, to see whether they are the employer of choice,
2. Upward feedback and company-wide employee surveys, to take the pulse of the organization and to "red flag" areas of concern, and
3. Turnover, especially of "star employees," which always signals a severe problem needing immediate attention.

## Summary

*If you want one year of prosperity, grow grain.*
*If you want ten years of prosperity, grow trees.*
*If you want one hundred years of prosperity, grow people.*
— Chinese proverb

It may seem obvious that retail success is completely dependent on superior people leadership, and yet so many companies fail

## AN INSIDE LOOK

## PEOPLES JEWELLERS – A NEW STRATEGY

When Clare Copeland stepped into the CEO role at Peoples, the focus had been on sales. Sales staff did whatever it took to sell, even if that meant heavy discounting. The management team believed that customers were price-driven but market research confirmed that management may have been too focused on price. Peoples discovered that customers valued professionalism and trustworthiness and thus a discount strategy was not a wise one.

Peoples hired many people from outside the jewellery business, invested heavily to develop a training program for its sales staff, and revamped its compensation scheme. As Clare Copeland explains, "It is so typical in retail to see a focus on sales rather than gross profit. We put bigger emphasis on not trying to beat last year's sales but rather to make planned gross profit levels. We realized that we were giving away margin, and so we changed our compensation system to focus on gross profits, not sales. Sales are nice to have, but you can't eat them." The right compensation plan was integral to Peoples' focus on its new strategy. The turnaround at Peoples has been spectacular as profits more than quadrupled the past three years under Copeland's leadership.

to invest the time on this key element. Fortunately, Canadian CEOs are starting to recognize the importance of employees. In the March 12, 1999, issue of *Canadian Business*, the number-two answer to the question, "What is your most important priority?" was "attracting and retaining high-calibre employees" with 23% of responses. The only higher priority was "increasing profitability," mentioned by 35% of CEOs.

**THE CHAPTERS' PERSPECTIVE**

# Employees First

Chapters places its employees first, and its customers second. The Chapters' stores with the highest sales increases year after year are those stores with the highest morale. Chapters has verified what other smart retailers have learned: employees who love what they are doing ensure a healthy profit margin.

## The Right Stuff

Like all champion retailers in search of people who will make happy, productive employees, Chapters looks for a positive attitude, including an open acceptance of people and a readiness to embrace change. The second attribute it seeks in candidates is specific to the book industry, a love of books. Chapters places high value on yet a third attribute – that of teamwork – since it is team-spirited people who ultimately move ahead into management capacities.

Using its own innovative interview process, Chapters seeks team players from the very start, beginning with the hiring process for employees. Two members of the management staff conduct a joint interview of about six to eight candidates. Within this social context they observe applicants' interactions with one another as part of the individual assessments. The process indicates each individual's social skills and comfort with teamwork, while he or she is being assessed for individual attributes.

Part of the magic of finding the right people is attracting the best candidates in the first place – individuals who would love to work in a national chain of booksellers, and who would thrive within the particular corporate culture. Word of mouth has proven to be one of the most reliable means by which Chapters has attracted such people. Management regularly asks the staff their feelings about working at Chapters, and their responses are heeded. This is one way that Chapters maintains its position as the most attractive place to work in the Canadian book-selling industry. Another way is the retail chain's emulation of a corporate outlook pioneered by Southwest Airlines, which embodies two main themes: that work should be fun, and that people are important. As a result, a steady

## Comp Store Sales Performance is Related to Staff Satisfaction

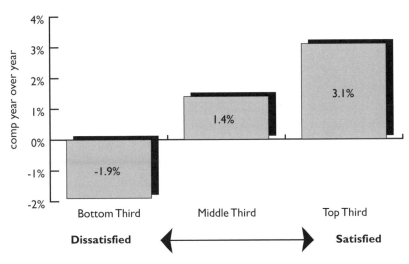

stream of applicants always exceeds the number of available positions at Chapters. As Andy Labute, Director of Human Resources, says, "We often receive 900 to 1,000 applications for 40 available positions when we open a new store."

In the beginning, promoting from within was a desired but unreachable goal. There simply weren't enough employees on the roster, given the number of stores that Chapters was opening, so senior store leaders came from other retailers to build a team that could grow with the company.

Today, talented applicants are readily identified and nurtured within the organization. But the company's commitment to promoting from within led management to establish a policy: if a member of the Chapters team leaves to join a direct competitor, the doors are closed against coming back. As Dan Soper, Senior Vice-President, Large-Format Stores, puts it, "We strongly believe that we should reward those who have stayed and helped us grow since they are the ones committed to our team." It is they who receive the reciprocal benefits of loyalty and support within the company.

## Training as an Incentive

Chapters invests heavily in training programs, which help to lay a sound foundation for the company while offering further incentives to employees. Introductory training in all the stores focuses on product and customer service knowledge to ensure that every new team member can successfully give the expected high level of customer service. People joining the Chapters family know they will have the opportunity to climb the ladder once they have demonstrated on-the-job competence.

After two years, employees may apply to take part in a formal training program called Master Booksellers in which they progress to the next level of expertise in sales, customer service, and product knowledge. The Chapters "University for Booksellers" trains employees ready to move up to management in the organization. Chapters has designed a college credit program for its employees with Ryerson University in Toronto, which now offers Canada's first B.A. in Retailing. As Mary-Alice Schmidt, Director of Human Resources for Large-Format Stores, says, "Chapters employees can now take three credit courses over the Internet from Ryerson – a truly innovative approach, with more than 100 Chapters employees currently enrolled."

The Masters in Bookselling Administration Program (MBA) is a four-day course of study designed for the top 100 managers. This training goes beyond bookselling into the development of problem-solving skills, and the analysis of strategies for given situations and available human and financial resources. This program operates every two years as new candidates are selected for this level of the organization. Executive staff also take specific training programs such as The Harvard Strategic Retail Management Program, with the objective of broadening the Chapters team with new ideas from other organizations.

## More Tools for Motivation

Chapters has undertaken several initiatives to motivate the entire employee team. There are 1-800 numbers for human resources and confidential issues. Climate surveys are elicited in stores across the country to get an accurate reading of employee perceptions, with plenty of room for feedback and recommendations for improvement.

Upward feedback at every level of the organization has also been instituted. Employees are encouraged to share their perspectives anonymously, so all supervisors have the opportunity to receive clear and confidential feedback as to how others perceive their leadership.

Social events bring people together in a more intimate way. "Town hall meetings" over a light morning breakfast, or beer and pizza, give employees the opportunity to have their questions answered by management about work concerns. New approaches are constantly created to celebrate exceptional performance in different areas, such as for delivering outstanding service at the store level, or reaching major milestones on a regional or national level.

A "Dream Points Program" allows each individual in the company to earn points for sales and service, and to redeem them for incentives such as a Chapters jacket or a microwave oven, all the way up to a mountain bike or a vacation cruise. Further incentives are offered each year for achieving the sales and performance objectives of the various stores. The winning team goes on the Big Apple Trip to New York to enjoy Broadway shows and fine dining, or to the Caribbean for a mega-celebration.

## *Well-Deserved Compensation*

Many of the company's top performers have seen their overall compensation increase over 50% in just four years, thanks to salary increases, bonus programs and accelerated promotions for outstanding performance. This reflects Chapters' belief that better compensation attracts and retains the best booksellers nationwide.

Bonus programs play a significant role in compensation. Quarterly and annual pay incentives are available to every employee, part-time and full-time, in stores that achieve their profit objective. Full-time employees receive full range of benefit packages, including university scholarship programs for their children. To attract the best part-timers, Chapters has a university scholarship program for part-time booksellers.

**Number of Chapters Employees
with Shares and/or Options**

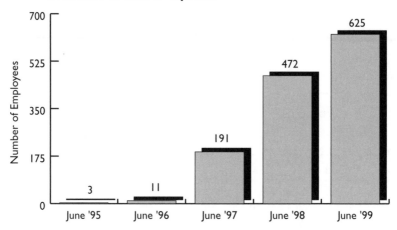

Chapters has designed an Employee Share Ownership Plan (ESOP). Employees may become shareholders in the company's public stock, through a payroll deduction plan at 15% discount off the market value, and in this way share direct ownership in the company. By becoming shareholders, employees benefit from their own competence and expertise, and the employee–customer relationship becomes all the more important to staff. Further, the top-performing senior employees – about 500 of them across Canada – are also eligible for options. While most organizations offer options only to top executives, it's a different story at Chapters. Virtually anyone at senior store level, including superlative-performance booksellers, may be issued options. Individual performance and day-to-day initiative in almost any capacity may be recognized and rewarded in this way. These programs help employees think like owners.

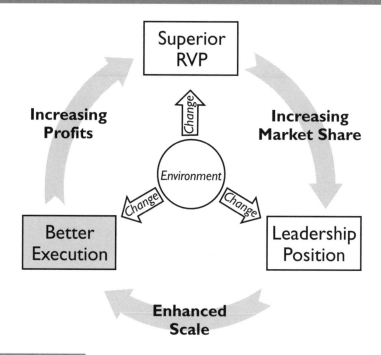

## PRINCIPLE 3:

### Execute better than competitors in the areas of people, technology and costs

***Chapter 5:*** INVESTING IN PEOPLE TO ACHIEVE CUSTOMER LOYALTY

1. There is a clear link between employee commitment and customer loyalty. Power retailers achieve customer loyalty by investing in their people.
2. They invest by hiring the right people, enabling them, and by motivating their staff through superior leadership, compensation, and constant celebration
3. Power retailers measure their return on people investment through objective feedback loops. This feedback guides continuous improvement.

***Chapter 6:*** MANAGING INFORMATION TECHNOLOGY FOR STRATEGIC BREAKTHROUGHS

1. Power retailers use information technology to manage merchandise selection and store planning.
2. They also customize their marketing using customer database management and innovative loyalty programs.
3. Information technology enables strategic breakthroughs such as Internet retailing.

***Chapter 7:*** COST MANAGEMENT TO MINIMIZE MARGIN EROSION

1. Managing costs is critical to maintaining sustainable advantage in a thin-margin business like retail. Power retailers focus on managing the key cost areas that most affect profits.
2. Power retailers manage and optimize their product category portfolio to maximize returns.
3. They share experience internally to continually improve, and also consider the entire value chain to look for economies beyond their business borders.

# 6

# Managing Information Technology for Strategic Breakthroughs

*"IT is make or break. If you're not good at IT, I don't think you can be good at retail in the long term."*

– Elliott Wahle, CEO, Dylex

The second critical aspect of successful execution is managing information technology (IT). This chapter will cover two of the important elements of execution highlighted by our retail CEOs, and outlined in Figure 6.1.

**FIGURE 6.1**

**The Key Elements of Retail Execution**

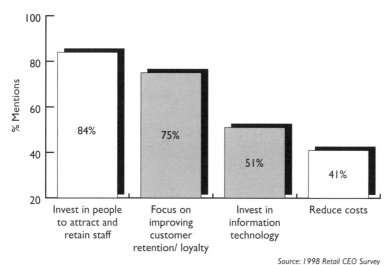

*Source: 1998 Retail CEO Survey*

Spending on retail IT has increased dramatically in the past few years. The Ernst & Young 1998 Canadian Retail IT Survey reported that spending on IT more than doubled as a percentage of retail sales over the period 1996 to 1998, as shown in Figure 6.2.

**FIGURE 6.2**

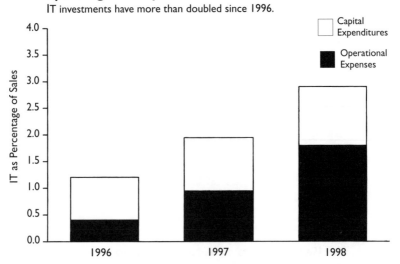

### Spending on IT by Canadian Retailers

IT investments have more than doubled since 1996.

Source: Ernst & Young 1998 Canadian Retail IT Survey

Although IT is a broad field, power retailers do three specific things with IT better than the rest of the retail pack:

1. they more precisely manage merchandise selection and store planning,
2. they use customer databases (including loyalty programs) to customize their marketing, and
3. they leverage technology to make dramatic business changes, such as the use of electronic commerce.

In other words, power retailers are using information to manage business details, to get closer to customers, and to innovate.

Power retailers know that managing information is not simply a technical matter to be handled by an Information Systems group; rather, it is of strategic concern to top management.

Information is not only a record of past conditions and performance, but more importantly, it facilitates better decisions about future resource commitments and activities. The central nervous system of any retailer, whether store-based or non-store-based, is the information system. As the cost of computer technology has dropped, there have been more and more useful applications for the retail industry. The single greatest driver of change in retailing over the past decade – and for the foreseeable future – is the widespread adoption of new methods of gathering, providing, and using information.

## Better Operations: Merchandise Selection and Store Planning

It was interesting that in our survey of retail executives about key areas of IT investment, "merchandise selection" received a score almost four times higher than the score received for e-commerce. Our survey is consistent with the research of others, such as Ernst & Young's 1998 Canadian Retail IT Survey. A long-standing and essential use of information technology is in managing product and store information to ensure operations proceed efficiently and effectively. While all retailers realize they need some method of managing their operations, the power retailers have adopted approaches to managing information that are at a micro level – at the individual SKU level, by supplier, store, customer, and sometimes even by shelf. Such data are in real time, accessible to all in the organization who need them, and presented in actionable formats. In short, power retailers totally integrate such information into the day-to-day operations of their companies. This allows them to

> *While all retailers realize they need some method of managing their operations, the power retailers have adopted approaches to managing information that are at a micro level – at the individual SKU level, by supplier, store, customer, and sometimes even by shelf.*

## RETAIL INFORMATION TECHNOLOGY – DRAMATIC CHANGES

By retail IT, we mean the use of technology:

- to acquire, store and retrieve, analyze, and use information about markets (e.g., customers, competitors)
- to develop and offer retail programs (e.g., assortments, advertising campaigns, customer retention programs, launching new formats such as Internet sites) and
- to improve the performance of those programs (e.g., by reducing inventory investment, and improving supply-chain management and service quality).

Broadly speaking, there has been a discernible progression in which aspects of retailing have been "informationalized," that is to say, more data-driven than ever before. A great deal has happened since the invention of the cash register in 1884 or even since the first optical scanner in 1961. In the 1970s, the focus was on automating operational tasks such as inventory control, accounting systems, payroll, and the like. The use of the computer was to do the same computational tasks, but faster and with fewer people.

In the 1980s, attention shifted to the supply chain to find ways to reduce inventory investments and replenishment cycle times. Efficient Consumer Response (ECR) became the objective of first grocery and then other mass merchandisers. The concept of "re-engineering" appeared frequently, meaning to find new ways to do things, not just doing the same thing faster or less expensively. Some retailers, particularly those in the food sector, quickly became very sophisticated users and leaders in retail information technology. Those chain retailers who have relatively low and stable SKU levels (stock-keeping units) were the first to adopt many computer-assisted technologies to make operations routine. Larger and more complicated retail operations (such as department stores) had a more difficult transition to make.

In the 1990s, attention again shifted. Increasingly, leading retailers moved from static, periodic reports to continuous on-line reports and customized queries. The drive was to move from data delivery to decision support. An assortment of management techniques such as category management and more efficient assortment became viable. Customer tracking enabled customer retention programs to move beyond the previous "buy five get one free" level. And the increasing acceptance of standards (for UPC, EDI, and much else) improved computer communications throughout the industry.

In North America and other parts of the world, leading retailers are treating point-of-sale monitoring (POS), just-in-time reordering (JIT), electronic data interchange (EDI), advance shipping notices (ASN), shared cheque authorization networks (SCAN), geographic information systems (GIS), loyalty and database marketing programs, and other information technology tools as the electronic vehicles for maintaining and expanding upon their competitive position. As these leaders get better and better at managing information, they are creating a shift in power in distribution systems from the manufacturers to the retailers.

As we enter the 2000s, we are seeing many instances of shortened, changed distribution systems (referred to as disintermediation) and foresee a continuation of this throughout the consumer goods industry. This means that we expect much increased attention to using the increasing bandwidth of telecommunications to bypass traditional retail distribution channels. As firms of all types adopt enterprise-wide information systems, their willingness and ability to reach out directly to consumers will increase. Wholesalers will get bypassed, as retailers get on-line. More companies will move to sell to the consumer directly.

---

make decisions based on timely facts, not simply on opinions and guesses.

The introduction of standardized individual SKU identification, bar coding (for scanning of items and containers), and advanced point-of-sale systems have enabled retailers to monitor item flow, to more effectively manage relationships with their suppliers, to ensure accurate reporting, and to develop customized, automated merchandise-management systems. For the industry leaders, every aspect of assortment management is now "informationalized" to optimize the productivity of inventories and store space. Initial planning of the assortment, order placement, delivery tracking, receiving, layout and shelf-space allocations, markdowns, transaction processing, and more are all built into assortment management systems. In each instance, information must be timely, accurate, detailed, and shared. These benefits in turn have helped retailers reduce inventory investments, reduce cycle times in the physical distribution system, and most importantly, move from "supplier push" to "customer pull" in their assortment decisions.

Loblaw is one of several industry leaders using information to enable efficient assortment. Efficient assortment refers to finding better ways to avoid unexpected inventory surpluses or shortages by tuning product flow to demand. This requires information systems and continuous communications to permit vendor-managed inventory and provides one's own staff with automated ordering, tracking, and receiving routines.

*Efficient assortment refers to finding better ways to avoid unexpected inventory surpluses or shortages by tuning product flow to demand. Information systems and continuous communications permit vendor-managed inventory and provides staff with automated ordering, tracking, and receiving routines.*

Assortment management techniques can be very data intensive and offer managers new and more numerous performance metrics. These new approaches tremendously increase the amount and frequency of information generated, processed, and shared amongst trading partners, and they speed up the cycle time for all assortment activities. For example, some retailers (usually of higher volume routine items) have moved from periodic replenishment systems to continuous replenishment systems, triggered by SKU tracking at point of sale and communicated directly to chosen vendors.

A new development for mass retailers is the notion of micro-merchandising their stores, either individually or by small regions. This approach is in contradiction to the "standardized planogram" issued by the merchandising team from head office. The micro-merchandising approach is to customize the assortment and customize the layout according to intimate knowledge of the local trading area and clientele. This requires information for the team onsite. It is not sufficient to vacuum up data at the

**AN INSIDE LOOK**

## LOBLAW COMPANIES – AN EARLY ADOPTER OF CATEGORY MANAGEMENT

Loblaw is Canada's leading grocery retailer with 1998 sales revenue of roughly $11 billion. The company operates a very efficient food distribution system, and its sales have grown by a compounded rate of 6.5% a year since 1990, more than double the industry average, with over 800 retail outlets (under a variety of banners) and approximately 5,000 wholesale accounts. Like most grocery chains, it operates on very narrow margins, which means that small changes in its cost structure can have major impacts on its profitability.

Loblaw was an early adopter of category management, which organizes its merchandising operation and is enabled by an extensive investment in IT. Category management involves dividing the merchandise assortment into groups, typically of items that go together from a customer's perspective, where each group can be operated as a strategic business unit (SBU), and thus judged on its profitability and contribution to the overall business. Loblaw's category managers are like general managers of their particular SBUs.

Each category manager has access to a great deal of data about each category. Sales in dollars and units, costs, margins, and more data by individual SKU make it possible for the category manager to calculate which parts of the assortment do what for total category profitability (using analytical management tools such as Direct Product Profitability). Such analyses of product movement and profitability inform future buying decisions.

Further, Loblaw's category managers build shelf plans using computer-assisted shelf management programs. These programs help decide what products should be put where. Loblaw's proprietary systems can track, analyze, and simulate product movement based on space allocations. This gives relevant product information for space allocation, but also shifts power from manufacturers to the retailer.

store level and send it all to head office; instead, the local store management team needs the information. The team needs to be enabled and empowered to be different from other parts of the chain, to be encouraged to engage in local marketing initiatives.

**AN INSIDE LOOK**

## LEVI'S – THE ORIGINAL SPIN PROGRAM

Levi Strauss sells jeans and sportswear under the Levi's, Dockers, and Slates names in more than 60 countries, with 1998 sales of $6 billion. Yet despite its size, Levi's provides an example of a retailer who uses information to customize its selection to individual customers. In 1994, Levi's launched its Personal Pair program in selected stores. Women were able to have themselves measured (the results were kept in a customer database) and a pair of jeans custom made. These jeans were delivered to the store in a week or two at a premium over purchase price of $10 to $15. The program increased repeat purchases dramatically and by 1997, 25% of women's jeans sales at Original Levi's Stores were through this program. In 1998, Levi's expanded this program to include men and a doubling of styles available. Under this new program, called Original Spin, the customer has input in the design of their jeans. Early results show great promise for this micro-marketing idea.

Among others, Dillard's Department Stores, Wal-Mart, and Sears are actively doing this. Sears CEO Arthur Martinez believes that although Sears is a national company, it should not be making merchandising decisions that way. As Jim Mergott, Sears, Director of Assortment Planning, says, "He wants the company to move away from what had become an entrenched national buying logic and make smarter decisions, store by store. We have to get much more market-specific."

"IT is very important to us," says Peter Vanexan, President of Grand & Toy. "While our business is simple, what makes it complex is the transaction complexity of six orders a second. If our computers don't work, we're in deep trouble. We work at tracking our customers. We track our products closely so when we sit with a vendor we know what's going on. We are changing our assortments, store by store, using computer-assisted planogramming. And we think of the Internet as just another way to deal with our customers. We even give our biggest customers special software so they can order directly from us using the Internet, saving time and money."

Power retailers use their retail information systems to manage a broad range of operations. Communications technologies have also enabled retail executives to stay in closer contact with their store operations yet reduce their travel time and costs. An executive can make changes system-wide within a matter of hours. Wireless technology has enabled store staff to be mobile within the store yet respond when needed. For example, Builders Square in the U.S. is using wireless telephones to enable on-the-floor sales associates to respond to incoming customer telephone calls.

## The Core of Data-Driven Retailing

For power retailers, at the core of data-driven retailing is the use of customer databases and related computer technology. The customer database is much more than a mailing list, much more than a map showing competitive locations. It is a computerized memory of everything that is known about customers and their individual relationships with the retailer over time. Each database is like an electronic filing cabinet of stored data which can be organized as the user wishes and updated as new information becomes available, and it can produce reports of answers to specific questions that the users ask. Using simple commands, the user can ask the software to locate specific records or to sort according to certain criteria such as "all customers who have purchased jumbo packages of diapers in the past week." These reports contribute to more effective decisions.

Data-driven retailing is not an entirely new concept or practice. Direct marketers, such as catalogue companies, record clubs, and credit card companies have been using databases for a long time. However, data-driven approaches allow huge retailers to do at an affordable cost what small retailers have always been able to do: to know their prospects, their customers, their competitors, and their trade partners intimately and then tailor their business accordingly. The implication of this is that large retailers can encroach upon one of the few competitive advantages remaining to small and medium-sized retailers: knowing their customers inside out. For example, a database enables the bellman at a Ritz-Carlton to review a daily printout of expected guests and their distinguishing characteristics so he can greet them by name as they arrive.

Prior to installing a sophisticated database system, American Express was limited to gathering such information as a card member's name and address, how long he or she had been a cardholder, and how much the card member had spent in the past year. With the implementation of a massive parallel processing system, AmEx was able to store information from every transaction that card members make, including the stores they shop in, the places they travel to, and the restaurants they eat in. AmEx uses this information to send offers to individual card members.

According to power retailers, the key to a successful data-driven marketing program lies not in the size of the database, but in the relevance of the data collected and the user's ability to work with the data. In many retail organizations, the most common lament of managers who have access to databases is that they have too much "data" but too little actionable "information." This is often the result of poor system design or inadequate training for users. It may also be the result of poor follow-through by senior management who should insist on getting value for their investment in data-gathering and processing. Power retailers have overcome these problems.

*A common lament of managers who have access to databases is that they have too much "data" but too little actionable "information," often the result of poor system design or their own inadequate training.*

As Christine Magee, President, Sleep Country Canada, states, "We use our databases in the store to look up product availability, to check on delivery routes and commitments, and to figure out the next available delivery time for the customer who is standing there in the store. It's part of what we can offer the customer. And we can check our database anytime to see who purchased what when, who dealt with the customer in the store, who delivered the bed to the customer, and so on."

While the principles of retail marketing have been known for

**BACKGROUND INFORMATION**

## RETAIL CUSTOMER DATABASES AND THEIR USES

### 1. Undertaking market research and experimentation:
- Which customers shop with us most often? What do they buy?
- Which catalogue layout worked better?

### 2. Market segmentation and loyalty programs:
- Which customers are most profitable and which cost us more to serve than we make?
- Communicating with loyal customers

### 3. New customers:
- Which customers are reducing their purchases with us? What can be done to reactivate them?
- What are the characteristics of our best customers?

### 4. Matching customers with products:
- Which products are most profitable and which least profitable?
- Are there cross-selling opportunities?

### 5. Develop models and forecasts
- What is the likely impact of a sales promotion based on past experience?
- When should markdowns be taken?

a very long time, retail marketing practice has recently been able to deliver much more completely on the admonition "Know your customer." The traditional methods used by retailers to get to know their trading areas and their customers – surveys, focus groups, and government census reports – provide relatively limited information relatively slowly. Power retailers now go much further, faster, and with much more accurate market assessment with geo-demographic and geo-psychographic market segmentation and customer profiling. To make these segmentation schemes geographic, retailers link data to either census geography or postal geography. When customer data are split into thousands of segments, it enables the retailer to "lower the microscope" considerably on the marketplace.

With the use of customer databases, and especially with the ability to integrate the information from several databases (called data enhancement), it is possible to build very detailed consumer profiles. For example, a retailer may develop detailed profiles of its major customer segments, which in turn helps its buyers and merchandisers. Better segmentation leads to finer-tuned demand forecasting, better trade-area analysis and site selection, and sharpened marketing programs. For example, Reader's Digest has one of the largest consumer databases – over 100 million families worldwide – which they use to create campaigns for their magazines, books, CDs, videos, and tapes.

All retailers want to know whether their expenditures are generating adequate return. Data-driven techniques help measure the exact impact of marketing activities, such as particular promotions to particular customers. It is now routine practice for leading retailers to measure traffic into their stores (or Web sites) and to calculate yield (the percentage of traffic that buys), and even to track which customers bought what and when. Electronic traffic counting helps a retailer know the impact of advertising and promotion or even changes in window displays and signs. Yield helps measure the impact of sales training, of incentive systems, the impact of labour scheduling decisions, and so on.

Mass retailers have long desired the ability to track their customers' behaviour in detail. While customer characteristics such as demographics and attitudes and intentions are all useful, knowing "exactly who buys what when" is invaluable for designing and adjusting a marketing program. Power retailers in particular have realized the potential of customer tracking through in-store POS and customer loyalty programs. However, the quantity of data that can be generated at this level of observation is staggering. For example, Wal-Mart tracks every transaction in every one of its more than 2,000 stores for more than a year. This tracking effort amounts to more than four billion rows of data and storage needs over five terabytes (that's five trillion). With this data, Wal-Mart, the retail industry leader, has been able to finetune its retail operations, thus constantly lowering costs and improving revenues.

Not only do power retailers track which customers buy and how much they spend and when, they also look closely at the contents of the "market basket." Market-basket analysis examines what is bought most commonly (Wal-Mart reported in October 1998 that bananas were the most common item in U.S. grocery

**BACKGROUND INFORMATION**

## COMMON DATA-MINING APPROACHES USED BY RETAILERS

1. Associations – What happens with what? For example, what products are typically purchased on the same shopping trip?

2. Sequences – How are events linked over time? For example, how long after someone buys a computer do they buy certain software or how long is the interval between purchases of an item such as laundry detergent?

3. Classifications – Can some marketing activities be classified as associated with certain kinds of performance? For example, are certain promotions, such as "buy one, get one free," more effective than other promotions across a wide variety of circumstances? Are some promotions more effective in stimulating traffic while others are more effective in improving yield?

4. Clusters – Are there groupings in the data? For example, do certain customers form segments that were not obvious before, such as customers sharing the same shopping behaviour?

5. Forecasts – Is it possible to develop predictive models of customers? For example, can one predict whether a customer who shopped in a store will continue to do so and for how long? Can lifetime value be estimated in advance? Can propensity to switch be forecasted?

## AN INSIDE LOOK

## WILD OATS MARKETS – TARGETING COMMUNICATIONS WITH PERMISSION

In 1987, husband-and-wife team Mike Gilliland and Libby Cook opened their first vegetarian health food store in Boulder, Colorado. According to their Web site, they feature organic and locally grown produce, chemical- and preservative-free groceries, hormone- and antibiotic-free meats, cruelty-free body care, and eco-household products. In 11 years, Wild Oats Markets has grown into the second-largest natural foods supermarket chain in North America with annual sales of about $420 million, with 68 stores in 18 states and British Columbia and an on-line shopping Web site at http://shop.wildoats.com. Sales for the first quarter of 1999 were $122.5 million, an increase of 34% over sales of $91.6 million for the same period in 1998.

Wild Oats recently began a loyalty program that allows individual customers to create and modify the electronic profiles Wild Oats keeps on each person enrolled. This "permission marketing approach" enables the company to send communications to each customer that are uniquely tailored offers. While the majority of loyal customers get paper mailings, as of early 1999, 22% of them chose to receive e-mail instead. And, rather than sending coupons, Wild Oats programs its POS systems to read the Wild Oats Shopper cards (or the special frequent-shopper key tags that are provided as an alternative to a wallet card). The POS automatically provides the special customized discounts on purchases that were promised by mail or e-mail to each customer.

carts) or what is bought with what. Using transaction records, typically stored in large databases, retailers use data-mining tools to seek patterns in their customers' shopping habits. For example, if purchasers of vanilla ice cream often purchase chocolate sauce, then the retailer may decide to cross-promote these items. Data-mining is a series of techniques designed to uncover non-obvious patterns in the data.

Power retailers use database analysis to make retail communications more efficient by reducing the waste that is so typical of mass-media retail advertising and direct-mail campaigns, by targeting different market segments with different messages.

Databases have played a major role in the rapid deployment of loyalty and continuity programs. For most retailers, it is more cost-effective to keep existing customers than to find new ones. Based on information such as spending volume, purchase frequency, and average order size, complex programs can be developed that reward the loyalty of one's best customers and sometimes reactivate lost customers. The essential idea is to do something to encourage further patronage and discourage defection to competitors. For example, Tesco, the leading U.K. supermarket chain, was reported in 1999 to have over 11 million cardholders in its program. Tesco creates more than 37,000 customer behaviour segments and rewards those customer groups separately with reward and incentive combinations for their patronage and doing such things as shopping at different times of the week and so on. Tesco uses its loyalty program to manage its customers, not simply to reward its customers for patronage.

While there are many dimensions to successful rewards programs, the role of information is pivotal. On the one hand, these programs enable a retailer to collect information that otherwise might not be available. For example, typically customers enrol in a program and at that time provide personal information that enables the retailer to profile its customer base. Further, at time of purchase, customers self-identify (in order to collect rewards), thus enabling the retailer to track purchasing behaviour and correlate it with personal characteristics and history. For example, Tesco analyzes the contents of more than 500 million shopping baskets a year to gain insights into its business. On the other hand, the information system must support these retention programs. Points or some other way of tracking purchasing history must be maintained for each enrolled member. Since most rewards programs involve the creation and distribution of some form of private currency (often points redeemable for merchandise or travel), the system must record and track each member over time. For example, Zellers' Club Z program has over 10 million members and each one is able to get an on-line update at a Zellers' POS.

# 12 CHARACTERISTICS OF SUCCESSFUL LOYALTY PROGRAMS

1. The program targets efforts disproportionately towards those customer segments that are most profitable, rather than against all customers.

2. Customers have the sense that the retailer is committed over time to reward loyal patronage (it's not a promotional gimmick).

3. There are both hard benefits (such as points for travel or merchandise) and soft benefits (such as recognition and special treatment). The rewards and recognition offered ideally are perceived to be of higher value by the customer than they actually cost the retailer to provide.

4. There are increasing discounts or rewards for patronage; that is, the more one buys, the better the treatment received.

5. The program is designed based on good research as to why customers stay with the retailer and why customers leave (rather than assumptions), so the program can powerfully stimulate frequency and amount of purchasing.

6. The program is easy and hassle-free for customers; for example, they can identify themselves easily even if they forget their membership card.

7. The program leads to personalization of relationship with the retailer.

8. The program is easy to administer (and thus costs are kept reasonable); for example, program procedures do not unduly slow transaction processing, and it is easy to process rewards claims.

9.  The program provides information on which individual customers purchased what and when (i.e., not an anonymous "paper card" program) so that a database can be created and maintained.

10. There is regular communication with program members (typically quarterly at least) as to status in the program, program news and changes, etc. There should be an opportunity for dialogue with program members, not just monologue.

11. The program is differentiated from other competitive loyalty programs in terms of features and benefits; it is not simply a "me-too" program.

12. The program builds upon a satisfying "core offer" to begin with, rather than being relied upon as the only reason for patronage. In other words, the loyalty program is "the icing on the cake."

As Ed Harsant, CEO, of Staples/Business Depot, says, "We have a Dividends program for our best customers. We key in their number at the cash register when they are checking out. We give them a quarterly rebate based on what they buy. The program gives us a lot of information on frequency of purchase, which particular products are being purchased by whom, the impact of our incentives programs, and so on. We use this to reactivate customers and to run special targeted promotions. And we look at the lifetime value of customers – we certainly want to keep our best customers happy." The micro-marketing enabled by data-driven techniques helps retailers uncover opportunities to cross-sell other parts of the marketer's assortment and thus increase the value of promising customers by "getting a greater share of their wallet." For example, some apparel retailers develop clientele records so they know what is in a client's wardrobe. Sales associates can then notify customers when new merchandise arrives at

*IT can be used to learn individual preferences, remember past purchases, speed up routine purchases, and otherwise customize the relationship with an individual.*

the store that complements past purchases, or suggest related items when dealing with a customer in the store. Power retailers such as Harry Rosen have learned how data can improve profits. Harry Rosen's "In-Store Retail Information System" is credited with increasing recency of customer visits by 58% and shortening the time between visits.

Databases (and data warehouses) can overwhelm retailers with information. A theme often repeated by retail leaders is that many people are experiencing great difficulty dealing with the volume of information presented to them – they want less quantity and more quality. Retail decision-makers have much more information today than their predecessors did, so they need new skills to deal with the deluge. However, power retailers have found ways to use customer databases to customize their RVPs to individual customers.

## IT and Electronic Commerce

IT has not only changed the way retailers manage their companies, it has changed the very nature of the retail industry. There are a number of interactive, information technologies that have created alternatives to traditional store-based retailing. The most noteworthy of these alternatives are electronic kiosks and the Internet.

Electronic kiosks and other interactive devices provide information and assistance and enable new payment systems such as debit and smart cards. For example, in categories as diverse as gasoline and wallpaper, sophisticated vending machines offer digital images of product assortment, touchscreen terminals, credit card acceptance, and for the retailer, database management. Such devices reduce the need for sales associates and enable new points of contact with customers. For example, in 1999 Sainsbury was rolling out touchscreen kiosks to 300 of its 400 U.K. grocery stores. These kiosks, called Reward Point units, are seven feet tall and three feet wide, located at the store entrances. These kiosks present ever-changing special offers to Sainsbury's 12 million Reward Card loyal customers. The kiosks are linked to the POS system and the Reward Card database so that different offers can be made to different customers.

Since 1995, Safeway U.K. has pioneered the use of self-check-out systems (they call it "Shop and Go") in more than 200 grocery stores. In 1999, Safeway launched a test of another IT initiative. Labelled Easi-Order, it provides frequent shoppers, free of charge, with a PalmPilot electronic organizer that comes with a built-in modem and scanner. Safeway helps customize the device with a suggested order based on past shopping history (derived from its loyalty card database). The customer can alter this personal shopping list at any time, using simple drop-down menus and the PalmPilot stylus. Safeway can also provide menu suggestions, ingredient lists, and simple advertising messages. The Easi-Order device can be plugged into any standard phone line and transmit an order to the store for pickup later, in this "Collect and Go" program. Home delivery is being considered as well. And, the customer can use the normal PalmPilot functions when not using the device for grocery shopping.

Electronic commerce has been receiving a great deal of attention in the media and the retail industry, attention vastly disproportionate to its achieved share of total retail sales to date. This attention is most likely due to the novelty of the retail approach and to the recognized potential this approach has for transforming the way retailers provide value to their customers, thus eventually threatening the mainstream retailing approaches of today. (This theme will be elaborated on in Chapter 8.) From an IT perspective, electronic commerce presents several opportunities and several challenges to retailers.

Electronic commerce entails a fundamental strategic change in the basic retail value proposition offered by most retailers today. Digital information allows new assortments, new kinds of convenience, new prices, and new experiences for the customer. For example, retailers can substitute information for inventory, Web sites for storefronts, e-mail for personal service, and pop-up graphics for media advertising. IT is critical to manage the

**BACKGROUND INFORMATION**

## 10 CHARACTERISTICS OF A GOOD RETAIL WEB SITE

A frequently asked question (FAQ) about Internet retailing is "What has been learned about the characteristics of a good Web site?" An effective Web site:

1. Enables a reasonably fast download of the home page. Also anticipates how customers may search for the site (e.g., key words likely used) and how search engines work (e.g., "meta-tags")

2. Takes advantage of the medium (i.e., serves not just as an electronic catalogue but is interactive (both within the site and through hot links to other related sites)) and is searchable

3. Provides value-added services (e.g., gift reminders, address finders, room design, menu suggestions, delivery tracking, customer help, links to other sites and so on)

4. Is fun and entertaining – offers games and other amusements to generate interest

5. Is changed frequently to keep it fresh (e.g., time-sensitive deals)

6. Provides relevant information (e.g., makes it easy to do side-by-side product comparisons)

7. Is easy to understand and to navigate

8. Reduces perceived risk (e.g., offers quality products, guaranteed delivery, secure payment options, privacy of information)

9. Makes it easy to buy multiple items (e.g., virtual shopping cart)

10. Enables the retailer to gather customer information in two ways: (a) obvious collection (e.g. surveys, billing information) (b) unobtrusive collection (e.g., source of enquiry, hits, pages visited, how much time spent and where on the site, etc.)

expanded assortment, to deal with the logistics of payment and product delivery, and to take full advantage of the opportunities to interact more richly with the customer. IT can be used to learn individual preferences, remember past purchases, speed up routine purchases, and otherwise customize the relationship with an individual. In short, IT enables the Internet to provide greater "reach" (contact with more customers) and greater "richness" (more depth and interaction in the relationship).

Electronic commerce, such as kiosks and Internet retailing, gives the customer much more control of the buying process by asking the customer to interact with the retailer's information. The customer may terminate the interaction at any time, leaving the retailer with little opportunity to recover. This is vastly different from the pervasive, intrusive, mass media advertising approach used by most retailers today and the legions of sales associates waiting for customers in stores.

## Summary

Managing information in retail is a daunting undertaking. It is expensive, time-consuming, and a constantly changing field. Done well, retail IT provides competitive advantage; done badly, retail IT can sink a firm.

According to those we interviewed, we will see a continued move towards distributed thinking and action as retail information is shared more broadly across the organization, rather than hoarded centrally or at the top of the management hierarchy. New analytic IT capabilities (mathematical models, forecasts, simulations) will help retailers answer the classic managerial questions: "What will be?" "What if?" and "What's best?" The power retailers have recognized the potential of IT to improve their performance.

## Leveraging Technology

In the Chapters environment, its information system is the central nervous system. The need for such a system was apparent in 1995, when SmithBooks and Coles were being united into one enterprise. One chain had an information system that tracked what it was selling, but not what it had on the shelf. The other chain had a system that tracked what was on the shelf, but not what it was selling. Both chains had only half of the information they needed to run a successful retail operation.

Over a period of three years, the two systems were unified into a cohesive whole, so that all the stores had both sides of the picture. But the problem was more complicated than that. Most retailers think of information systems as having three parts: sales at the front end (or the point-of-sale system, in the form of cash registers), an inventory system, and a back-end or back office system, which links to other networks such as an ordering system, a distribution centre, and a financing system. That's the standard retail set-up.

At the time of the merger, information was so compartmentalized between the two chains that, rather than having the standard three systems, there was a total of 14. Three years of painful consolidation weeded out the duplications and inconsistencies and brought the number down to five. These were the dedicated point-of-sale and inventory management systems used by both the small and the large stores, and one back-office system that linked to each of these. Much of the initial investment was devoted to reducing the needless complexity.

As Harry Yanowitz emphasizes, "Systems was the one area where we dramatically increased our spending post-merger, because we believed we would not be a world-class retailer if we didn't invest to arrive at the leading edge of technology." The end result is a retail operation that knows what it sells, knows what is on the shelf, knows what needs back-ordering, and is in its best in-stock position ever – including at such hectic times as the Christmas season.

The original stores that merged into Chapters usually were out of stock in 13 to 15% of their bestsellers. Roughly 5% of this total were "natural out-of-stock" titles – books that publishers hadn't yet reprinted. In the best possible situation, book retailers are normally out of only this 5% at any given time. Within four years, as a result of the now-comprehensive information system, the out-of-stock position was reduced to 7 or 8%, cut almost in half. Computerized feedback enabled higher sales, a better in-stock position, and increased inventory returns due to identifiably unpopular and slower moving titles. All of this served to reduce the working capital requirement, increase sales, and increase profitability.

## *The Loyalty Program*

Chapters' innovative use of information systems is most readily apparent in its enormously sophisticated and successful loyalty program. Chapters has the largest paid loyalty program in Canada today, with close to 700,000 members across the country. The program was made possible only through the investments that the company made in its computer network, and it has come to assume a core role in Chapters' ongoing marketing program.

While each cash register records the titles of books sold, it also links each sale to each customer who belongs to the loyalty program. Not only does Chapters know that Book "A" sold in store 123 on December 5, it also knows that John Smith bought it. It is the purpose of the loyalty program to link these two pieces of information.

Chapters' computer-enabled loyalty program was preceded by other redemption programs that could only target customers at random. A "shotgun approach," such as blind circulation of inserts in local newspapers, generally drew a redemption rate of only 1 or 2%. This is in great contrast to Chapters' tailored Avid Reader and Chapter 1 mailing programs, which average an 8% return. Some redemptions have gone as high as 15%, virtually unheard of in direct marketing.

The loyalty program is based on the belief that not all customers are created equal. When Chapters first launched its loyalty program, it did so after having discovered that 22% of its customers represented a full 58% of its sales. This realization led to a drive to reward these customers in order to control two primary variables, retention rate and share of wallet.

These two variables have enormous impact over a 10-year period. With an average 75% retention rate, and a 30% share of wallet, a customer is worth $250 in profit over 10 years. With a powerful loyalty program, if the retailer can move the 75% retention to 90%, instead of losing one out of four customers every year it will lose only one out of ten. Boosting the retention to 90%, and the share of wallet to 90%, increases the value of an average customer from $250 to $3,000. This is the economic logic of the Chapters loyalty program. The absolute best customers – the upper 22% – increase Chapters' profits through their loyalty to the company. Chapters pampers these customers to reward and encourage their loyalty.

## *How the Loyalty Program Works*

Chapters' sophisticated information system is an enabler. The customer information in itself is not what makes customers loyal; what makes them loyal is the variety of programs that are matched to their interests, as indicated by their purchases.

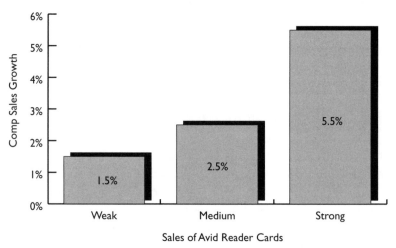

**Impact of Avid Reader on Sales**

Comparative Same Store Sales vs Avid Reader Sales

Chapters' mall stores have offered loyalty programs (called Avid Reader) longer than the large-format stores (called Chapter One), so they are most appropriate to use as a case study. In the mall stores, customers pay fifteen dollars for a 10% discount on all their book purchases for a calendar year. On any dollar spent on any product – books, greeting cards, magazines, newspapers – they receive what is called an Avid Reader point. When 200 points are accumulated, the customer is mailed a five-dollar coupon, applicable towards any purchase. Every 100 points received afterwards generates yet another five-dollar coupon. A heavy buyer will effectively on the margin earn a 15% discount. The Avid Reader program benefits anyone buying in excess of $150 of books a year.

In the second year, the plan is renewable for ten dollars rather than fifteen, to encourage customers to remain onboard rather than letting their membership lapse. The point of Chapters' loyalty program is to change customers' behaviour. Prior to using the Avid Reader card, best customers of Chapters bought 33% of their books from the chain. After purchasing the mall store Avid Reader card, Chapters' share of wallet soared to 77%.

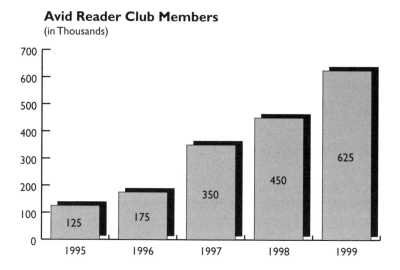

**Avid Reader Club Members**
(in Thousands)

Consumers perceive great advantages in loyalty programs. The above chart illustrates the popularity of Chapters' loyalty programs. Beginning with 125,000 members in March of 1995, the number more than quadrupled over a four-year period.

The Chapters loyalty program was designed so that the effective discount progressively increases with the amount of dollars spent, as shown in the chart below. Buying a few books a month earns a good discount, and buying more books earns an even better effective discount.

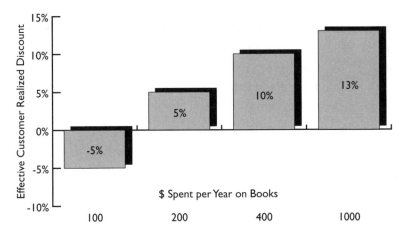

**Heavy Book Buyers Earn Higher and Higher Effective Discounts**

So higher spending leads to higher discounts. But as David Hainline states, "Our loyalty programs are more than just discount programs. They help us identify, develop, serve, and retain our best customers." Chapters' investment in technology has also enabled it to be a pioneer in Canadian e-commerce, a story we will return to in Chapter 8.

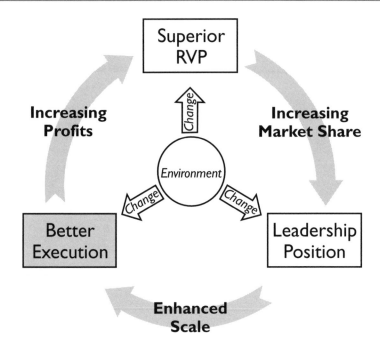

---

## PRINCIPLE 3:

## Execute better than competitors in the areas of people, technology and costs

### Chapter 5: INVESTING IN PEOPLE TO ACHIEVE CUSTOMER LOYALTY

1. There is a clear link between employee commitment and customer loyalty. Power retailers achieve customer loyalty by investing in their people.
2. They invest by hiring the right people, enabling them, and by motivating their staff through superior leadership, compensation, and constant celebration
3. Power retailers measure their return on people investment through objective feedback loops. This feedback guides continuous improvement.

### Chapter 6: MANAGING INFORMATION TECHNOLOGY FOR STRATEGIC BREAKTHROUGHS

1. Power retailers use information technology to manage merchandise selection and store planning.
2. They also customize their marketing using customer database management and innovative loyalty programs.
3. Information technology enables strategic breakthroughs such as Internet retailing.

### Chapter 7: COST MANAGEMENT TO MINIMIZE MARGIN EROSION

1. Managing costs is critical to maintaining sustainable advantage in a thin-margin business like retail. Power retailers focus on managing the key cost areas that most affect profits.
2. Power retailers manage and optimize their product category portfolio to maximize returns.
3. They share experience internally to continually improve, and also consider the entire value chain to look for economies beyond their business borders.

# 7

# Cost Management to Minimize Margin Erosion

> *"We have to make sure that we maintain our cost advantage versus our competition. Scale is a huge advantage for us, and that means everything from buying product, such as a Citizen watch, through to purchasing boxes, on which we spend $5 million each year."*
> – Clare Copeland, former CEO, Peoples Jewellers

Forty-one per cent of our retail CEOs identified cost reduction as one of the key elements of successful retail execution. (See Figure 7.1.) Power retailers know that in their business, costs must fall continually, and ahead of prices, which are difficult to hold steady. In fact, winning retailers understand that if managing costs is not high on the strategic agenda, margins will erode, perhaps fatally.

Managing for profit – driving out non-value-added costs and knowing precisely where the money is made – is necessary for success in retail. The reality is that retail margins are thin, and in many categories are getting thinner. In fact, the average U.S. general merchandise retailer's gross margin fell by 5 full points between 1986 and 1997 (from 34% to 29%). In Canada, similar pressures exist: sales per employee across all retail categories is essentially flat. Between 1975 and 1997, sales per employee grew by less than 3% over the entire 22-year period. This translates into a pathetic 0.1% gain in productivity each year. Senior executives know that they have to do better. "In the old analogue world, 6% productivity [growth] was magical," says Paul Allaire, Chairman and CEO of Xerox Corp., quoted in *The Wall Street Journal*, February 2, 1999. "In the digital world, if you don't have double-digit productivity numbers every year, you're going to be out of business."

**FIGURE 7.1**

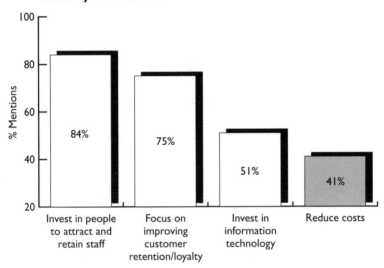

The Key Elements of Retail Execution

*Source: 1998 Retail CEO Survey*

And with intense competition, too much shopping space, the rise of the Internet and of the category-dominant retailer, the pressures on retailers' margins are likely to increase even more.

For power retailers, cost reduction is familiar territory. They know that they are gone if they don't manage every nickel, every minute detail of their business. At Home Depot, Executive VP and Chief Administrative Officer Ron Brill handled all of Home Depot's non-retail product purchasing (things bought for Home Depot's use, not for sale). Brill outlawed fax machines and photocopiers from all stores, until the mid-1990s. If anyone in a store needed to send a fax or make a copy, he or she used Kinko's. A store would not be given approval for these two pieces of equipment until its revenue grew to more than $40 million. While this might sound extreme, it is an illustration of how cost-conscious winning retailers are.

Power retailers do three things well:

1. They manage their product portfolio to first determine and then optimize their returns.
2. They share experience within their operations and continually benchmark against leaders.
3. They look beyond their business borders to consider the entire value chain (the entire system), from manufacturing through to delivery and after-sales service.

## Beginning with Product Line Profitability

Power retailers determine exactly where they make, and don't make, money. While this sounds straightforward, collecting the data, analyzing it, and achieving consensus to act on its implications are complex undertakings.

Most retailers, when looked at by product category, exhibit a pattern similar to that shown in Figure 7.2, which highlights a typical set of issues for retailers, using disguised data for a department store:

• A small percentage of revenue and of shelf space accounts for the vast majority of direct product profits. The 80/20 rule (80% of profit comes from 20% of products) is seen everywhere in retail, whether selling food, drugs, apparel, or giftware.
• Gross margin and direct (full) profit are often unrelated. What may show up as marginally profitable using only gross margin, can be unprofitable on a fully loaded basis.
• For many retailers, square footage is allocated to product without using direct profit as a guide, resulting in too much space for unprofitable product categories and not enough for the real stars.

**FIGURE 7.2**

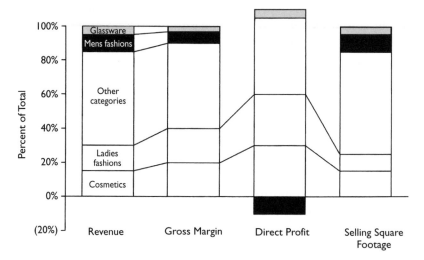

### Revenue, Profit and Square Footage – Typical Situation

Power retailers go the extra mile to ensure that they have a full and complete grasp of profitability by product category, including all related costs (from advertising to merchandising to labour to carrying costs to management attention). They use this information to optimize their stores' space allocation to maximize overall profitability.

Power retailers ask two questions for each product category:

1. Does it make money on a fully-costed basis?
2. If not, is it a draw for customers? (Even if it loses money, maybe the category is needed to attract customers as a classic "loss leader" or as part of a shopping trip for more profitable product.)

Figure 7.3 outlines one way to think about the intersection of these variables. When arrayed on a matrix as in Figure 7.4, a given retailer's strategic priorities emerge:

**FIGURE 7.3**

## Product Line Profitability Decision Framework

Decisions on specific sub-departments are made by combining customer draw and shopping-basket profitability.

*Shopping-basket profitability*
(stand-alone profitability + cross-sell profitability)

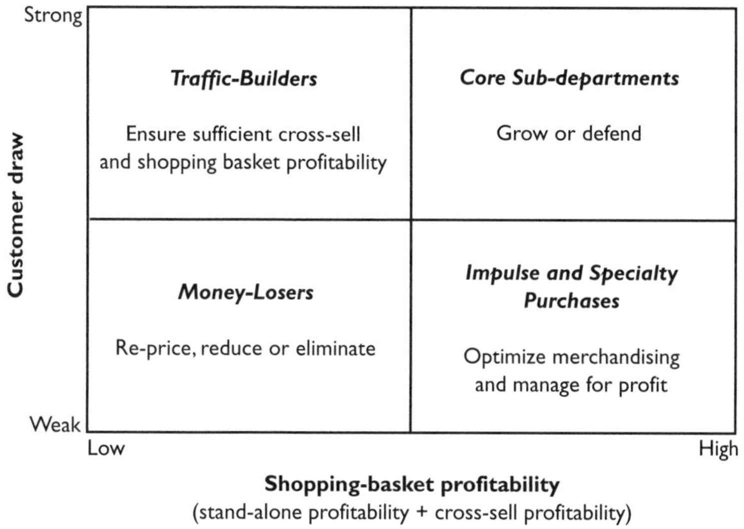

1. *Core sub-departments:* With their high profit and large draw, these departments are the foundation of the business. Any gains here have the potential to dramatically improve the fortunes of the business. Any losses to competitors in these categories could be catastrophic.

2. *Traffic-builders:* These are the true loss-leaders, drawing lots of customers, but are not being cross-sold well enough to justify the strategy. People are coming into the store, but they aren't buying other products. Square footage should be reduced for these categories, or they should be re-priced to make them profitable or re-merchandised to make them better cross-sell candidates.

3. *Impulse and specialty purchases:* These are categories that are core sub-departments in the making: they are extremely profitable but lack shelf space and sufficient category dominance to "draw" customers to the store.

4. *Money-losers:* These are neither unprofitable nor a customer draw – in effect, these categories do nothing but hurt the retailer's P&L and customer equity. They should be either re-priced to make them profitable, reduced in terms of space allocation, or eliminated from the store altogether. The typical retailer has many of its departments in this quadrant, which could be reduced to reallocate space for the potential future core sub-departments.

## FIGURE 7.4
### Product Line Profitability

Product categories A and B are traffic builders, but not part of profitable shopping basket (space should be reduced and prices increased). O, P, Q and S should receive more space, while F and G must be defended. Categories in the lower left require dramatic changes to pricing, merchandising and space allocation.

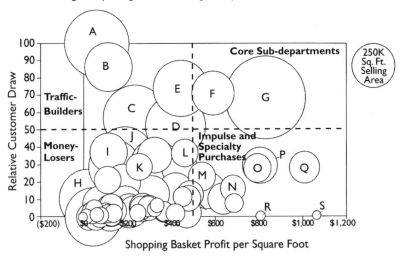

## Managing Costs by Benchmarking

Most retailers have an enormous advantage over other businesses when trying to improve performance: they may have dozens, even hundreds, of locations, each serving as a "unique" business, doing some things well, others poorly. BDP (Best Demonstrated Practices) is a benchmarking process that shares the learning that is already present in the retail organization.

There are two categories of BDP, internal and external. Internal BDP allows retailers to examine all the stores within the organization, in order to implement the best practices currently in use. External BDP looks at what the competitors are doing and implements their best practices, which provides a healthy reality check for the internal BDP targets. Gathering data for internal BDP is very easy. However, the results gained from it are those of continuous incremental improvement. In contrast, gathering the data to determine external BDP is much more difficult (as shown in Figure 7.5), but the intelligence gained can lead to quite dramatic improvements.

**FIGURE 7.5**

### Internal vs. External BDP

Internal BDPs are more straightforward to conduct than are external BDPs, but they tend to lead to less dramatic, though often significant, change.

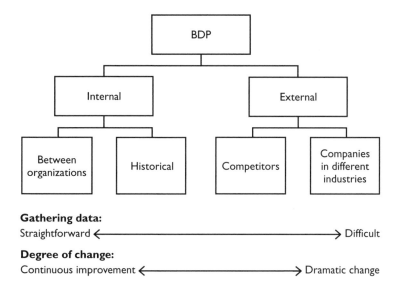

## Internal BDP

Internal BDP is all about sharing best practices within the current operations, and is an ongoing process among power retailers. Based on the identification of the most profitable stores, internal

*An internal BDP identifies the most profitable stores within an operation with the idea of learning and then sharing their "secrets" to high profitability with other less profitable stores in the system.*

BDP focuses on a thorough examination of their operations. Their secret to high profitability should be replicated in all other stores. Having said this, no one store is typically the best at everything: even the most profitable store can be made better through BDP.

Power retailers base internal BDP on data-focused comparisons, which take into account variables of similar qualities and characteristics so that organizational apples are compared to other apples and not oranges. There is probably no use comparing a store in Grand Prairie with one in

## FIGURE 7.6

### BDP Analysis

Doing an Internal BDP analysis involves several steps.

| Process Step | Key Success Factors |
|---|---|
| Select comparable organizations for BDP | • Stores should be comparable, operating under similar conditions |
| Disaggregate organizations into major processes | • Lay out major (3–5) processes |
| Construct first-cut BDP | • Gather data<br>• Identify best practice organization for each process |
| Construct adjusted BDP | • Adjust data for uncontrollable elements (e.g., labour rates, product mix) to ensure an "apples-to-apples" comparison |
| Quantify impact | • Calculate potential impact (revenue increase or cost savings) by unit and by process |
| "Peel the Onion" in leveraged areas | • Focus on organizations & processes with most potential<br>• Determine drivers of differences at a more disaggregated level |
| Develop an action plan | • Set a BDP target<br>• Establish a detailed schedule<br>• Assign responsibilities |
| Implement | • Obtain commitment at all levels of the organization<br>• Communicate goals, deadlines and responsibilities<br>• Celebrate successes along the way |

Toronto; comparisons should be drawn among stores of similar size, location, competition, and demographics, assessing raw performance by removing uncontrollable variables like dissimilar real estate costs.

The methodology should focus on controllable elements that will have the biggest impact. Power retailers are very good at developing a laser-like focus on the most important cost areas, then actively managing them.

It is important to realize that performing an internal BDP analysis takes time and requires several detailed steps. Figure 7.6 shows the eight steps typically taken to determine the best practices to identify those with the greatest potential for revenue increase or cost reduction, and to set up an action and implementation plan.

## SWISS STORES–BDP IN ACTION

**AN INSIDE LOOK**

Swiss Stores (disguised name), a large department store chain with a strong foothold in Europe, had experienced rising sales, general and Administration (SG&A) costs for more than five years. The company had been trailing far behind market leader Marks and Spencer in the United Kingdom and needed to improve its cost structure to compete more aggressively.

In order to achieve cost-structure improvements during an 18-month period and to reduce the workforce by 10 to 15%, Swiss Stores used Best Demonstrated Practice (BDP) analysis to quantify potential gains in operational efficiency. The analysis was based on an analysis of 60 stores with a comprehensive, onsite review of 92 sales/support activities. The focus was on defining future performance objectives based on the best results within each activity.

The BDP analysis found potential cost savings of $30 million per year. It also identified a potential 9% reduction in current salary costs and a potential 12.5% reduction in full-time employees. Based on these findings, Swiss Stores was able to prepare action plans for each store detailing organizational changes, cost savings, and the roll-out (implementation) schedule. It had achieved $20 million of savings by the end of 18 months.

### ■ *External BDP*

An external BDP exercise is similar to the internal process, but allows a retailer to identify answers to questions such as: What do we pay versus the competition? How many non-store staff should be on the staff team? What is the revenue per non-store employee and per store employee and how does this stack up with the best competitor?

In conducting an external BDP exercise, power retailers focus on areas where their competitors excel and where they know, or sense, that they perform relatively poorly.

The process completed, retailers often find themselves overwhelmed by the wealth of good ideas, and don't know where to begin applying them. Power retailers avoid this confusion by using a potential-impact bar-chart, as shown in Figure 7.7, and a priority matrix, Figure 7.8. With the priority matrix, retailers can quickly decide those actions that have both a high dollar impact and a high likelihood of implementation. These are the areas that deserve undivided focus. These actions should be quickly assigned to senior managers with all the necessary authority to make the changes happen fast.

**FIGURE 7.7**

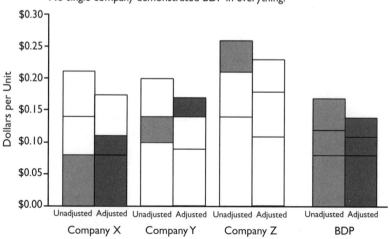

**Potential Impact, Adjusted BDP**
Shading indicates which piece had the best performances.
No single company demonstrated BDP in everything.

**FIGURE 7.8**
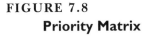
**Priority Matrix**

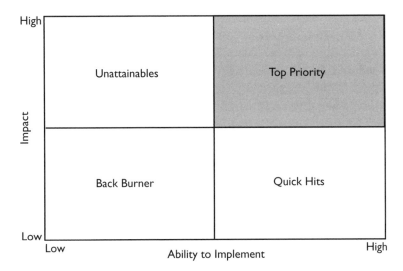

## ◼ *External BDP and Relative Cost Position (RCP)*

Relative Cost Position (RCP) analysis builds on the information yielded by an external Best Demonstrated Practice analysis and helps retailers to quickly get to the heart of any cost advantages that their competitors may have. It will also help them to formulate answers to both strategic and tactical questions and point to those areas where early action will reap the most benefits, as shown in Figure 7.9.

Power retailers know that it is not a simple task to gather the data necessary to determine their cost positions relative to the competition. Some of the data may be available in published reports but much of it will require extensive research and interviews. Figure 7.10 lists some of the data sources, highlighting the fact that the puzzle of RCP is put together from many different figures, no one of which will produce the entire answer.

**FIGURE 7.9**

## Relative Cost Position

RCP analysis helps answer both strategic and tactical questions.

| Strategic questions | Tactical questions |
|---|---|
| • In what areas do our competitors have the biggest cost advantage? <br><br> • What is driving competitors' profitability? <br><br> • How much flexibility would our competitors have in a price war? <br><br> • What is our market position? <br><br> • What are the strategic implications of the full potential cost position? | • Where should we focus our cost reduction efforts (e.g., wage rates, cost of goods)? <br><br> • Which cost elements would decrease significantly with an increase in scale? <br><br> • Which cost elements might benefit from different business practices? |

*(Copyright © 1998 Bain & Company, Inc.)*

There are two approaches to understanding a company's relative cost position and a combination of the two is most popular with retail winners. The faster method (though a less accurate one) is to adopt a top-down approach, comparing the competitors' cost structures at a macro level to one's own. Through an examination of the major cost elements, the retailer can determine the key differences between its processes or business practices and those of the competition. The retailer can then make some assumptions about its competitions' relative cost impact and test the assumptions against the competitors' overall financial data which are publicly available. While this quick method is indeed less accurate than the one described below, it identifies the cost areas of significant focus and is especially valuable in cases requiring some quick action to improve performance.

The second and more accurate approach is a detailed bottom-up analysis, which examines each major cost element for key competitors. This method uses cost data from multiple sources to arrive at an accurate picture of each competitor's cost structure, as shown in Figure 7.11.

## FIGURE 7.10

### Relative Cost Position Data Sources

Multiple data sources should be used whenever possible

## FIGURE 7.11

### Costs per Basket of Goods – Relative Cost Position

Using a variety of sources, the picture of RCP becomes clear by comparing costs amongst retail competitors. Both Company H and Company I would lose money on these transactions.

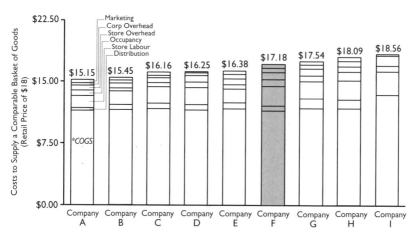

*Note: COGS includes discounts

With limited resources, a compromise solution for relative cost position analysis is to use the quick method and test the findings with a more detailed approach for one or two of the key cost elements.

### Managing the Entire Value Chain

Having performed an internal and external BDP exercise, power retailers turn to the next area of potential savings: the entire value chain, as outlined in Figure 7.12. Whereas BDP optimizes only the retailers' own operations, Value Managed Relationships (VMRs) look beyond the retail operation to optimize the entire system, and is often known as Efficient Customer Response (ECR). Power retailers realize that while they have actively pursued cost reduction for some time, they have begun to reach diminishing returns, and that the best opportunities for going forward require them to search for value beyond their own business boundaries. Thus, retailers need to look outward in the value chain and incorporate wholesalers and original product suppliers into their thinking. Armed with this perspective, power retailers use new technology to make it happen.

**FIGURE 7.12**

**The Retail "Value Chain"**

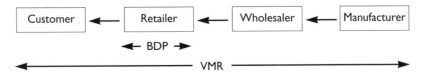

### Value Managed Relationships

Value managed relationships offer retailers phenomenal benefits – one study estimates the average savings from fully implementing VMR at 4.6% of sales – but it is the most complex cost-saving, quality-enhancing approach, requiring a true partnership to be formed between retailer and supplier. Having said this, VMRs are virtually immune from competitive raids, because these partnerships are typically long-term and company-specific.

The first step and most important part of successful cost reduction through VMR is to pick the right partners. These suppliers should be similarly cost-conscious, managing efficiently, be very reliable and show a willingness to look for opportunities to share information and grow profits. They need to think about their business – and their relationship with the retailer – in a new way.

VMR represents a new way to do business for retailers – it focuses on growing the total value pie, not on who gets what part of the existing one. Colonial Merchandise (disguised name) was a ladies' apparel chain with high costs which resulted in a severe margin squeeze. BDP wasn't enough to turn around Colonial's profits, so Colonial management looked beyond their business borders for savings. To reduce the total value chain, Colonial management first identified major suppliers. More importantly, though, management also identified the low-cost/high-quality suppliers amongst these large vendors.

*Value managed relationships offer retailers phenomenal benefits. The first step is to pick the right partners. These suppliers should be similarly cost-conscious, managing efficiently, very reliable, and looking for a way to share information and grow profits.*

The next step was to perform some fundamental analyses on these companies, to understand, for each:

- its cost structure, components of costs and trends
- its capacity utilization
- its other major customers

Armed with these facts, Colonial management could determine which subsets of its supplier base to align with, factoring in:

- which vendors could supply Colonial with additional product. (If a vendor was already supplying Colonial with cotton shirts, at what cost could it produce adjacent products, such as cotton T-shirts, sweaters or other cotton merchandise?)

## WAL-MART AND PROCTER & GAMBLE— FROM ZERO-SUM TO VMR

Wal-Mart is Procter & Gamble's biggest customer, representing about $3 billion of sales to Procter & Gamble. P&G and Wal-Mart have had a typical retailer–supplier relationship in the past, with no information-sharing between the two. "We let our buyers slug it out with their salesmen," said Sam Walton, Wal-Mart's founder.

But today, Wal-Mart and Procter & Gamble have formed a true partnership that is focused on system savings. P&G essentially controls Wal-Mart's P&G inventory, and receives real-time data on P&G's sales inventory and prices by store from Wal-Mart. This allows P&G to produce to demand, determine specific quantities for particular stores and ship directly to Wal-Mart stores.

To the shoppers, this system's inventory savings are passed on in lower price points and virtually no stock outs.

To P&G and Wal-Mart, not only are sales up, but costs are down even more, as order processing, billing and payment functions have been eliminated, and P&G sales representatives can visit Wal-Mart less frequently than before. This relationship of trust and information-sharing has clearly led to benefits for Wal-Mart, and Procter & Gamble as well as their customers.

- which vendors would benefit most from increased scale, by Colonial consolidating its purchases with them. Which had the greatest amount of spare capacity, and would marginally-price the next orders? Which could utilize less-productive labour (including inefficient processes and procedures) better than the others or had spare capacity which could be used more effectively?

- which supplier could be most helped by a change in timing, frequency, or quantity of orders from Colonial. Instead of monthly production and shipments, could system costs be saved by combining orders, ordering less frequently or holding some additional inventory? Would the benefits of longer production runs outweigh this additional carrying cost?

The spirit of all of these questions, and of many others, was that these were opportunities to improve the system, without worrying about who got what portion of the savings. In this case, Colonial agreed with its vendors (it reduced its vendor count by 60%) to share any and all sys-

*Power retailers have learned to continually work on cost reduction initiatives. They know that these initiatives never really end, that there are always more savings to achieve, and that once goals are met, the bar must move up.*

tem savings 50/50. So both parties had a phenomenal incentive to look for benefits throughout the entire value chain. As a result, two years later, Colonial's cost of goods was reduced by almost 10%, which dramatically turned around its margin squeeze.

## Cost Reduction Initiatives Never End

Power retailers have learned to continually work on cost reduction initiatives – from internal and external Best Demonstrated Practice to Relative Cost Positions to Value Managed Relationships. They know that these initiatives never really end, that there are always more savings to achieve, and that once goals are achieved, the bar must move up.

They also separate the visible from the invisible. Reductions in store labour, since they will be felt by the customers, are often the last place these retailers look for cost savings. In areas like real estate, cost of goods or overhead, though, there are invisible opportunities that the customer will never really see. David Bloom, Shoppers Drug Mart's CEO, says, "You have to always remember that there is no cash register in the boardroom: it's all about supporting what happens in the store – corporate is only a cost centre." The theme of "invest for customer loyalty and run lean everywhere else" is a popular one amongst the power retailers.

## BACKGROUND INFORMATION

## BEYOND BDP AND VMR: FULL POTENTIAL TOOLS

No one cost-reduction tool is a cure-all. Not every retailer can accomplish every objective. Some tools, like BDP and RCP, help get the organization moving quickly. VMR is a long-term set of focused initiatives that needs senior (often CEO-level) involvement, as it represents a fundamentally different way to do business. Other tools, such as experience curves or zero-based budgeting, help set specific targets.

Many different tools can be used to manage costs and achieve full potential, as shown in the table below:

| Technique | Complexity | Generate Ideas | Help Set Specific Targets | Compare With Self | Compare With Competitors | Measure Customer Value |
|---|---|---|---|---|---|---|
| Best Demonstrated Practices | | | | | | |
| – Internal | Low | ✓ | ✓ | ✓ | | |
| – External | Medium | ✓ | ✓ | | ✓ | |
| Experience Curve | Low | ✓ | | ✓ | ✓ | |
| Zero-base Budgeting | Low | ✓ | | | | |
| Value-chain analysis | High | ✓ | | ✓ | ✓ | ✓ |
| VMR | High | ✓ | | ✓ | ✓ | ✓ |
| Complexity Reduction | Medium | ✓ | | | ✓ | ✓ |
| Product-line profitability | High | ✓ | ✓ | | ✓ | ✓ |
| Cycle-time Reduction | Low | ✓ | ✓ | | ✓ | ✓ |
| Outsourcing | Low | ✓ | ✓ | | | ✓ |
| Overhead Value Analysis | Low | ✓ | ✓ | | ✓ | |

## Summary

Cost reduction is an ongoing priority for power retailers. They realize that controlling costs – especially "invisible" costs – allows them tremendous flexibility to out-invest the competition in many areas, from IT to labour. They use a variety of tools to keep costs at the top of the strategic agenda, including benchmarking, Value Managed Relationships, and product line profitability, which is as much a management technique as it is a cost reduction tool. Power retailers use these tools to solidify competitive advantage.

# *The Neverending Saga of Cost Reduction*

**THE CHAPTERS' PERSPECTIVE**

Chapters has found from its inception in 1995 that the business of cost management is a neverending saga.

In the Canadian book industry, gross margins declined from 37% in 1993 to 33% in 1998, an event driven by three pressures. Number one was the general growth of bestseller discounting and loyalty programs, which effectively meant that the best customers were getting discounts in bookstores across the board, including in the smaller bookstores. During this same period, large-format stores were on the upswing, operating at a 4 to 5% lower gross margin than the small stores. Finally, substantial share gains were made by deep discounters of books – companies such as Costco, Wal-Mart, and the grocery chains. As these outlets gained share at a lower gross margin, bookstores had to find cost savings of 4% of sales just to stay even on a profitability basis.

Since 1995, Chapters moved to reduce costs in four key areas. The first was in its support-office costs. These costs were defined as everything "above the store." Since the merger, Chapters managed to reduce its retail support office costs by two full percentage points in its first four years of operation. Given that net income margins as a percentage of sales are themselves under 2%, this reduction in support office costs was a key requirement to ensure continued and sustained profitability.

Another area of reduction was in rent, as a percentage of sales. First of all, unprofitable stores that had an unacceptably high rent-to-sales ratio were closed. As Chapters Vice-President of Real Estate Larry Balaban states, "Closing 190 of our 440 mall bookstores over the past four years has not made us popular with mall owners, but as a direct result, today we have a strong portfolio of profitable mall bookstores. They will be a core part of our business for the next quarter century."

An important part of this picture was that the burgeoning large-format stores, with a lower rent-to-sales ratio, gained an increasing share of the market. The combination of closing high-rent stores and opening more lower rent-to-sales ratio superstores improved the profit margin by one full percentage point.

Chapters also zeroed in on savings in labour costs, especially in the mall stores, whose efficiency could be benchmarked to other similar operations. By benchmarking these outlets, while conducting studies of other like-size stores and scheduling more efficient labour hours, Chapters was able to boost all of the underperforming stores to the average of all stores in labour costs.

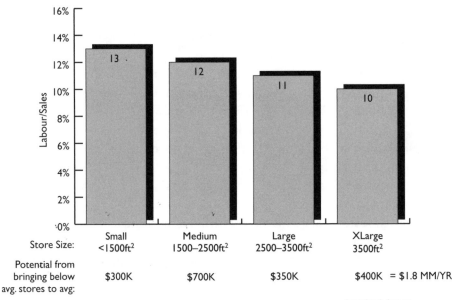

**Mall Stores – Labour BDP Analysis 1992 – Divided by Store Size**

| Store Size: | Small <1500ft$^2$ | Medium 1500–2500ft$^2$ | Large 2500–3500ft$^2$ | XLarge 3500ft$^2$ | |
|---|---|---|---|---|---|
| Potential from bringing below avg. stores to avg: | $300K | $700K | $350K | $400K | = $1.8 MM/YR |

*Source: Bain & Company*

As Sarah Strachan, Senior VP of Mall Stores, said, "A disciplined approach to scheduling labour hours not only has helped us manage our costs, but by having staff on the floor at the right time, we have been able to improve our sales performance."

Distribution presented its own set of problems. The question was how to distribute a continuous stream of books, in large and small quantities, without the distribution costs becoming prohibitive. The primary answer was in Chapters' expanding on the use of its own distribution facility in Brampton, Ontario. In this way, larger shipments could be consolidated from the company's self-amassed stock, and be sent to each store at one time. Further, the freight costs themselves decreased, since Chapters' freight costs from its own distribution centre were below those of all publishers. By reconfiguring these logistics of distribution, Chapters found yet another way of significantly reducing its costs and increasing its margin of profit. As Dennis Zook, the President of Pegasus Wholesale Inc., says, "Being a scale player allowed us to save considerable costs in shipping books to the stores."

## A Glimpse Into the Future

Chapters projects that in the next five years retail gross margins for books will decline by a further 3%. Different game plans will be needed to counter the expected new trends. Large-format stores will continue increasing their market-share gains, as will non-traditional book retailers such as warehouse clubs. Finally, the explosion of lower-price Internet sites is expected to make up at least 15% of the book business by the year 2003. Chapters will continue to focus on reducing its costs to improve the company's profit margin.

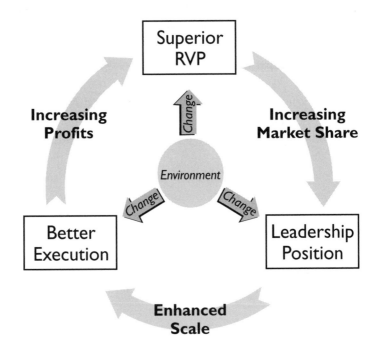

---

## PRINCIPLE 4:

### Lead change by continually reinventing the organization

**Chapter 8:** Anticipate to Lead Change

**1.** Adhering to the first three principles will lead to success in the short term, but ironically may lead to long-term failure because success often breeds complacency and resistance to change.

**2.** Power retailers anticipate and lead change and follow six steps to constantly reinvent themselves.

**3.** Retail faces continuous environmental change – the Internet represents a cataclysmic change. All retailers must develop an Internet strategy to deal with this tsunami.

# 8 Anticipate to Lead Change

> *"Any retail business created before 1997 is going to be a fossil by the year 2010."*
> – Len Riggio, Chairman and CEO, Barnes & Noble

Abiding by the first three principles does not guarantee that a retailer will successfully implement this fourth principle for success. Retailers clearly need to develop a winning retail value proposition (RVP), establish clear market leadership, and execute superbly. But, ironically, the retailer who religiously follows the first three principles for success is more likely to violate this last one, because changing a successful organization is often more difficult than changing one that is in turmoil. It is perhaps the most difficult principle to follow – yet without a strategy for leading change, the retailer will in fact be a victim of change.

The power retailers lead change. They know that while historical success is no guarantee of future success or even survival, change is a certainty. They embrace change, they know where the organization is going, when to bring new players onboard, and how to stay focused while responding to change – and sometimes this means reinventing themselves before the deck is on fire.

The first three principles outlined in the first seven chapters of this book need to be constantly re-evaluated in the light of environmental changes. Customer needs change, competitor strategies and business definitions change, often overnight, and the winning strategy or RVP that has the company buoyant today may sink it

## SEARS IN THE U.S. – MAKING THE TOUGH DECISIONS

Under the leadership of Arthur Martinez, Sears', operation in the U.S. has experienced a truly remarkable turnaround.

In the 1960s, Sears was the U.S. retail powerhouse – in 1964, Sears was bigger than its five nearest competitors combined. But over the next 25 years, Sears lost its way. It diversified into non-retail sectors, as it failed to recognize the market changes that called for a refocus of its retail value proposition. Sears' market share had dwindled as specialty stores and category-killer stores stole into the sector along with the new entrant, Wal-Mart. By 1992, Sears was experiencing the worst year in its history. The company lost $3.9 billion on sales of $52.3 billion.

Martinez articulated a very clear and different vision for Sears, one that built upon its strong brand name. Sears had been known for all of its house-brand, such as its appliances and hardware, but Martinez envisioned Sears as a fashion category-killer. He emphasized the "Softer Side of Sears" and almost all of his actions were completely consistent with this new view: to be number one in the customer's mind in the fashion category and number one in market share in a correctly defined market.

Martinez brought in an entirely new management team, some of them from other retailers and some from non-retail sectors – all of them very bright, very motivated, and supportive of his new direction. He also made some tough decisions. He closed 113 stores and closed down the very core of Sears – its 101-year-old catalogue business, an institution that had had its day and was now losing more than $100 million a year.

While Martinez made the tough decisions in order to change the direction of the organization, they proved to be the right decisions. The momentum of his new vision gathered as his newly renovated stores quickly outperformed the other stores, thereby justifying the new direction for the entire organization. New compensation plans rewarded the people who were heading in the new direction with him. Increased employee training allowed staff to deliver on this vision. The overall result? Sears went from a loss position in 1992 to earning more than $1 billion in 1998. Sears must now again reinvent itself if it hopes to maintain the momentum.

Paul Walters has worked similar magic with Sears Canada. He adapted many of the Sears U.S. initiatives and was able to improve profits from a paltry $9 million in 1996 to an impressive $146 million in 1998.

tomorrow. As Clare Copeland of Peoples Jewellers observes: "All strategies eventually fail. Retail markets change very quickly and this means we're constantly aware that our strategy may have to change."

There have been some very successful retailers whose strategies clearly reflected that they had followed the first three principles for years, and who have spiralled downwards simply because they ignored this fourth principle. Sears had been by far the preeminent discount department store in the U.S.A., but suddenly nosedived when Wal-Mart, a major player in the discount department sector, seemingly came out of the blue to dominate that market. What was Sears' strategic weakness? Rather than changing the focus of its RVP and reinvesting in its stores and people, Sears had ploughed the profits from what had been a very successful discount department store and catalogue business into insurance and other unrelated products. It soon faced its worst year in its history. But before it spiralled out of existence, new leadership took Sears in a new direction. By applying the fourth principle, CEO Arthur Martinez reinvented Sears and took it from a losing proposition to the number-one position in its sector today.

> *Following the three principles is not enough. Power retailers know that in an ever-changing retail environment, it's essential to be adaptable, creative, and ready to reinvent oneself and embrace a new vision.*

The Sears story is the stuff of retail legend. Roots is another example of a retailer that has been able to successfully reinvent itself. Roots initially started out as a trendy shoe retailer. Recognizing that the negative heel fad was passing, Roots reinvented itself as a brand for the hip and in achieving this new vision became emblematic of a lifestyle.

The Gap is another example of a power retailer that has adapted in the face of change. Founded in 1969 in San Francisco, The Gap's initial RVP focus was to serve the "generation gap," the baby boomers then in their teen years, with a variety of jeans, especially Levi's, and a limited selection of casual, functional "basic

## EATON'S – THE LOST GENERATION

AN INSIDE LOOK

No company better demonstrates the impact of failing to change than the venerable Eaton's chain, one of Canada's oldest retailers. Founded by Timothy E. Eaton, the first T. Eaton & Co. store opened in Toronto on December 8, 1869. Throughout most of the 1950s, 1960s, and 1970s, Eaton's dominated the Canadian department store sector. In 1993, the Retail Council named George Eaton, Distinguished Canadian Retailer. Yet by 1997, Eaton's was forced into bankruptcy under Companies' Creditors Arrangement Act (CCAA) and in 1998 lost $72 million.

Why? Simply stated, the market had changed; Eaton's had not. One customer's take on the store's demise was recently quoted in the *Globe and Mail*: "When my grandparents used to give me pyjamas, they always came from Eaton's," she said. "I associate this store with their generation despite the renovations." Since 1989, 34 U.S. retailers have set up shop in Canada and invaded Eaton's product categories. While specialty retailers and category-killers increasingly devastated many of its key product lines, Eaton's did not invest its profits back into its stores.

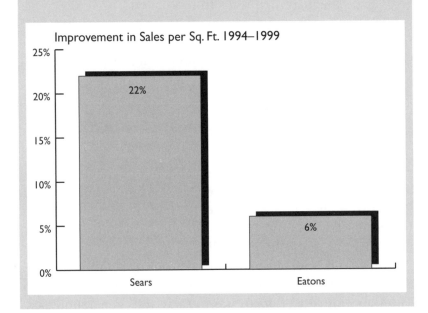

Improvement in Sales per Sq. Ft. 1994–1999

Eaton's downward trajectory is a classic example of failing to adapt the first three principles in the face of massive environmental change. For the last five years, Eaton's has been unable to improve its sales per square foot, while over the same period its direct competitor, Sears, has been able to improve its sales per square foot by 22%.

By 1999, Sears' sales per square foot productivity exceeded Eaton's by 64% – an enormous gap. Unable to drive sales, by 1996 Eaton's was the fifth-largest department store in Canada and, even excluding the discount department stores Wal-Mart and Zellers, it had sunk to a number-three slot in mainline department stores. In four short years, Eaton's had lost half of its market share.

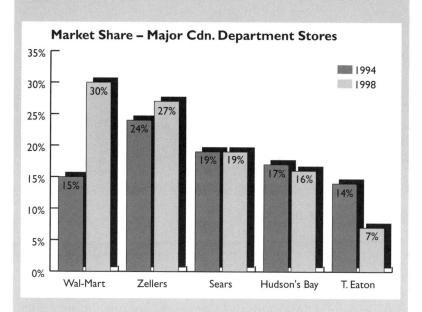

**Market Share – Major Cdn. Department Stores**

K-Mart was absorbed by Zellers in 1998 and this acquisition, combined with the success of Sears and the expansion of Wal-Mart, has left Eaton's in a difficult and precarious position. As Jack Welch, the legendary head of GE, said, "If the rate of change inside an organization is less than the rate of change outside, the end is in sight."

And for Eaton's the end appears to be here, as it announced that it was filing for bankruptcy in late August 1999.

with attitude" clothing at moderate prices. Thirty years later, with the boomers now pushing fifty, The Gap has had to readjust its focus and respond to the ever-changing market by broadening its assortment and its appeal. By doing so, it continues to attract today's teens but has not forgotten its original customers, their "boomer" parents. New lines, higher price points, fashionable advertising, more stores, and above all, a strong focus on associating its brand with a contemporary "cool" lifestyle image, have all contributed to its remarkable success.

### Changing Within a Changing Environment

Power retailers keep all four principles in mind when defining and implementing strategic directions and, when necessary, are prepared to reinvent themselves in response to changes in the market.

And for those who violate the first three principles? In general, these retailers are unwittingly *forced* to reinvent themselves – without a focused strategy for change. The recent bankruptcy of Eaton's is a most striking example. Eaton's has undoubtedly been forced to change by virtue of its having violated several dimensions of the first three principles, but was unable to change sufficiently in time.

## ■ *The Only Constant Is Change*

Change is not unique to this era; it has always been a driving force in our economy. Consider that in the early 1900s, 85% of workers were in agriculture; today less than 3% of the labour force works in agriculture. This change happened over seven decades and has caused enormous dislocation. At the turn of the millennium, the issue is not change itself but the rate of change – today change happens more quickly than ever before.

Things change so rapidly in our world, in part because new communications technologies provide tremendous opportunities. The Internet, which we will return to later in this chapter, is but one of the manifestations of the exponential rate of change. In just seven years, the Internet has spread to a quarter of the population. In contrast, it took 13 years for cell phones to reach

**FIGURE 8.1**

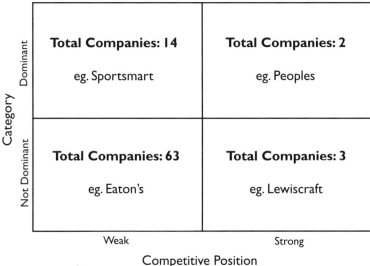

## Canadian Retailers – Gone or Restructured

|  | **Weak** | **Strong** |
|---|---|---|
| **Dominant** | **Total Companies: 14**<br><br>eg. Sportsmart | **Total Companies: 2**<br><br>eg. Peoples |
| **Not Dominant** | **Total Companies: 63**<br><br>eg. Eaton's | **Total Companies: 3**<br><br>eg. Lewiscraft |

Category

Competitive Position

the same level of penetration, 16 years for PCs, and 34 years for VCRs.

In retail, this means that new retail concepts, new things that consumers see when they are travelling in other parts of the world, can almost overnight become new demands that customers place on their homegrown retailers.

While some retailers have outpaced the competition, others have simultaneously floundered in their wake. Over the past 10 years, some 82 major Canadian retail companies have gone bankrupt, restructured, or disappeared altogether. As illustrated in Figure 8.1, all but two of the 82 violated our first two principles. Fully 80, or 98%, of these retailers did not dominate their market or they did not design a winning retail value proposition. The two exceptions, Peoples Jewellers and Steinbergs, had to restructure as a result of enormous debt loads arising from leveraged buy-outs. A full 77% of the restructured or lost retailers violated both of the first two principles.

## Strategies for Leading Change

How then to avoid the fate of the 82 retailers covered in the matrix? The key is to successfully reinvent the organization as the environment changes. In our research, we identified six key elements for successful change initiatives:

1. Collect data on an ongoing basis from key stakeholders, especially customers.
2. Establish the need for change. Share the facts throughout the entire organization.
3. Articulate the vision for the future.
4. Inject the organization with new blood that will champion the new direction.
5. Orchestrate a few early wins to convert fence-sitters to embrace the new direction.
6. Align incentives, performance evaluations, and rewards with the new direction.

### ▉ *1. Collect Data on an Ongoing Basis from Key Stakeholders, Especially Customers*

The first, and often the most critical step, is to hear and see problems and opportunities before it's too late. The retailer needs to establish a radar system to pick up the early signals. Management also needs to face "facts" rather than view the world as it used to be or as they would like it to be.

Rick Maurer, the author of *Beyond the Wall of Resistance* (Bard Press, 1995) emphasizes the importance of setting up "feedback loops" to direct an organization towards the need for change. He gives an example of an organization that is traditionally very resistant to change – a hospital. To stay attuned to processes and procedures that require change, the hospital uses feedback loops to measure itself on three key elements:

- clinical outcomes,
- customer satisfaction, and
- financial performance.

Similarly, retailers need to establish feedback loops. One objective measure is obviously financial performance. Systematic deteriorating profit clearly indicates a need for a change. But financial measurement must be augmented with customer and employee feedback loops as well. Financial information, after all, is a result of a retailer's actions – customer and employee data help predict performance.

## ■ *2. Establish the Need for Change. Share the Facts Throughout the Entire Organization*

Convincing people of the need for change is relatively easy if the deck is on fire, but ideally change should occur before the need is obvious. Martinez inherited a burning deck at Sears, which was an obvious impetus for change, but Wal-Mart changes constantly, even as profits grow healthily. It is imperative to help people understand the need for change and to recognize that those who resist change often do so simply because they do not understand the reasoning behind the initiative and its direction. While these resisters may feel at first that change is not good for the organization, they will support the idea as they come to understand where it will lead. When given the facts and knowledge that convince them that the change is good both for the organization and for them personally, many, but not all, resisters will willingly convert to support the new strategy.

## ■ *3. Articulate the Vision for the Future*

Successful change requires strong leadership to communicate a vision for the future which is energizing and credible. Power retailers develop a very clear vision of where the organization wants to be and then communicate this vision throughout their entire organizations. The changes needed to achieve this vision cannot be successfully implemented until every individual has a clear understanding of what that vision is and why the organization is heading in that direction.

### ■ 4. Inject the Organization with New Blood that Will Champion the New Direction

As David Stewart, the former CEO of Marks & Spencer Canada says, "If you can't change the people, change the people." Inject new blood that is fully supportive of the new direction. Otherwise, it will take so long to affect change that the resisters will actually win. Changes that should have been successful will be undermined by a majority of people who might, in fact, want to stop that change. The organization needs to move quickly to remove indomitable resisters. The management team that designed the previous strategy can sometimes be the staunchest resisters, perceiving any changes to that strategy as a personal affront to them. Almost anybody who has experienced successful change realizes that there are always some that are dead-set against the new plan, regardless of how well the vision is communicated throughout the organization. At a certain stage, the organization must deal with these individuals. If they cannot be brought onside, they cannot be part of the go-forward team.

### ■ 5. Orchestrate a Few Early Wins to Convert Fence-Sitters to Embrace the New Direction

Power retailers structure the process to ensure a few early wins. Essentially, this is the strategy that will convert fence-sitters to the new direction. Clearly, there will be setbacks along the way. For this reason, people need to build confidence on successes that happen early in any change process. Doubters and resisters are more likely to convert when the strategy produces measurable and visible wins right from the outset. As more wins occur, the new direction gains greater momentum. Everyone's commitment grows as more and more people begin to think: "Yes, this is a great idea! I want to be part of this winning team!"

### ■ 6. Align Incentives, Performance Evaluations, and Rewards with the New Direction

Finally, power retailers overhaul their organization's performance-measurement and management-compensation systems. A key step in motivating individuals to implement change is to develop a new performance-management system that will allow people to understand the new goals, objectives, and values and that rewards them for achieving these targets. One of the best innovators in the world, 3M, pays a bonus that is tied only to new products from the previous three years. Incentives drive continuous innovation at 3M. Rewards could entail a number of incentives such as job promotion, increased compensation, or individual employee recognition. Employees need to see the rewards not only in the dollars of compensation but also in terms of job recognition. It is important to ensure that others within the organization see that those who have chosen to head in the new direction are, in fact, receiving the right recognition for their commitment and ability to change.

A corporate culture that is willing to experiment must also be willing to throw sufficient resources behind new ideas. Even more important, it must protect those people that fail when they try those experiments. Taking risks always involves an element of failure. Whether in science or business, trying new things will, initially, produce a higher failure rate then remaining with the status quo. But success over the long run depends on many short-term

**FIGURE 8.2**

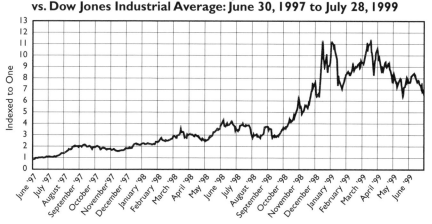

Relative Performance of the Dow Jones Internet Commerce Index vs. Dow Jones Industrial Average: June 30, 1997 to July 28, 1999

FIGURE 8.3

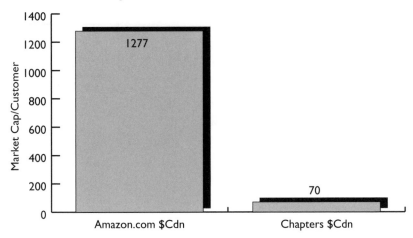

## Market Capitalization/Customer

failures and the learning that accompanies this trial and error. Employees have to be fully supported in their efforts to try new ways of doing things.

### Tackling the Internet Challenge

Retailing has been characterized by constant changes:

- in applying old ideas to new businesses, such as when Staples used the food supermarket concept in office products
- in applying new ideas to old businesses, such as when King Kullen pioneered the self-service grocery store
- in applying new ideas to new businesses, personified by eBay conducting virtual auctions on the Internet

Such changes can be cataclysmic, such as the malling of North America and the subsequent explosion of power centres. The current and foreseeable cataclysmic change is Internet retailing, enabled by information technology, and changing so quickly that writing anything about it in a book is indeed a risky proposition.

Retail change has been driven by real estate during much of this century. Department stores moved from the downtown core to the suburbs in the 1960s, '70s, and '80s, driven by the malling of North America. Real estate has also been the driver of the migration from malls to power centres over the past ten years. In Toronto alone, 2.8 million square feet of big-box retail space was built in 1998.

The Internet will irrevocably change the way people shop in the years ahead. Retailers who fail to change with this new environment will wake up to find their customers drifting away. The market has clearly decided that the Internet is the future, as shown in Figure 8.2.

Another way to look at how the market has valued the Internet is to look at the market capitalization per customer (the value that the market places on the company for each unique customer relationship) for Amazon (an on-line book retailer) versus Chapters (primarily a bricks-and-mortar retailer) in early 1999, as shown in Figure 8.3.

Thus the market values each Amazon customer close to 20 times more than it values a Chapters customer. With the market valuing each customer this way, which of the two companies can afford to spend more to acquire a new customer or to keep an existing one?

More than half of all Canadians now have Internet access (either at home or at work) and as they get more and more comfortable with issues such as credit card security, the volume of on-line transactions will explode. On-line retailing jumped from $3 billion in 1997 to $7.1 billion in 1998 and is projected to grow to more than $40 billion by 2002 as shown in Figure 8.4.

The Internet provides several dramatic advantages to customers that the brick-and-mortar retailer cannot match such as:

1. *Convenience:* The customer can now order from the comfort of home at 2:00 a.m. or on Christmas Day. For the time-starved customer, a five-minute shopping trip on-line often beats a drive to the mall to search the shelves. For instance, compare

FIGURE 8.4

### Internet Shopping is Showing Exponential Growth

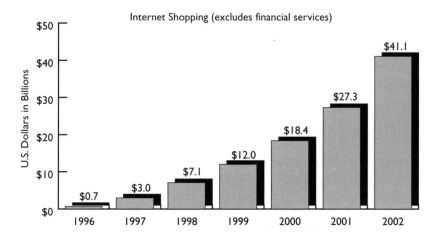

Source: Jupiter Communications

the convenience of buying a book as a gift for someone in a different town on the Internet versus in a store. Chapters.ca will wrap your gift and send it to the recipient, saving you a trip to the store and the post office. Bridal and gift registries will do well on the Internet. Related to convenience is the consumer benefit of speed. The consumer can quickly check for best prices and availability, without visiting four or five stores. They can then checkout effortlessly because all their information is on file.

2. *Selection:* No bricks-and-mortar retailer can carry all the SKUs in its category. The largest Chapters stores carry 130,000 book titles, but there are close to three million books available on Chapters.ca. Virtual Vineyards, an on-line service for the epicure, allows browsers to buy not only wine but also smoked salmon, caviar, rack of lamb, Belgian chocolates, or mango cilantro chutney. The Internet is also perfect for hunting down

rare or collectible items such as a particular baseball card or a vintage automobile.

3. *Price.* The Internet will be the cheapest source for some products. Banking and financial services should be much less expensive on the Net given the low relative costs for banks to handle transactions in the virtual market versus through bricks-and-mortar outlets. (See Figure 8.5.)

Price will also be a factor at auction sites, sites driven by advertising revenue, and sites that carry products which have no value once time elapses (i.e., airline tickets, concert tickets, hotel rooms). Given that comparison shopping is only a click away, the consumer rules on the Internet, especially when it comes to commodity items available from numerous sites.

4. *Personalization:* The Internet is the ultimate one-to-one marketing vehicle. It even welcomes customers by name like the great Ritz-Carlton doormen! This personalization adds tremendous value for the consumer. A site need not tell customers about specials a customer doesn't care about. The site can show only clothes in sizes and styles that match clothes a customer

**FIGURE 8.6**

**Internet Banking is Cheaper for Banks**

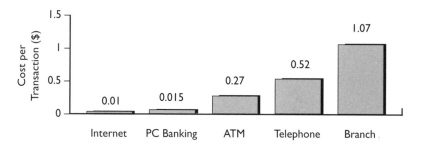

*Source: Booz-Allan & Hamilton*

has already bought, or can recommend books based on books that were loved by other readers. A site that has mastered personalization can offer a customer his or her own shopping assistant.

5. *Unique Functionality:* The Internet can provide functionality that is just not available in the bricks-and-mortar world. At Chapters.ca customers may search the book universe by subject category or key word, which would be impossible in one of the physical stores. Booksites provide customer reviews, bestseller lists for hundreds of book categories, and can send e-mail to let you know when favourite books are coming out. LandsEnd.com lets customers build their own model (including hair and skin colour, height and body shape) to allow them to quickly try on hundreds of outfits without ever seeing a changing room or breaking into a sweat. Lands' End's "Your Personal Model" was developed by Public Technologies Multimedia (PTM) of Montreal, and allows shoppers to save their "model" for future visits to the site.

> *The Internet is a vehicle to sell more products to customers, but it can also provide information, be used as an advertising venue, and allow your customers to give feedback on products and service.*

The Internet is obviously a vehicle to sell more products to the customer but it is more than that. It can also:

- Provide information to customers. Sites can display store locations. The Internet can advise of new products, or provide product ingredient information, including availability of existing products. As shown in Figure 8.6, many products are researched on the Internet, but purchased through other means. If a retailer is not on the Web, it is missing this golden opportunity to drive traffic to its stores.
- Be used as an advertising vehicle. This is a lower cost means of advertising to customers than traditional advertising and flyers. Canadian Tire has very effectively tackled this with its Web site.

## GARDEN.COM – LEVERAGING INTERNET CAPABILITIES

One Web site that is providing unique functionality is Garden.com. Garden.com, an on-line retailer of nursery and garden products, is leveraging the capabilities of the Internet. Garden.com is competing in the $43 billion U.S. gardening market which is highly fragmented with few known national brand-names. Garden.com also accepts phone and fax orders. The site has rich and relevant content thanks to numerous partnerships. For example, Horticulture On-Line provides much of the site's content. Continually updated content gives surfers a reason to come back to the site. The site provides a gift registry and a Gardener's Forum. Ninety per cent of its orders are drop-shipped from suppliers, so it carries little inventory and yet has access to over 15,000 SKUs. The site provides ultimate selection in a convenient and personalized way. Garden.com is targeted at the growing customer segment who want to do it themselves but don't have the time. Garden.com provides a "solution," thanks to garden planning software that allows customers to input their own garden details. Garden.com then can help plan the perfect garden, sending the appropriate products at the appropriate time (when they should be planted in the customers' garden given their local weather conditions). To top it off, Garden.com sends e-mail to tell customers how to take care of what they have bought.

• Serve as a communication vehicle for customers. Internet accessibility gives frustrated customers an outlet, which leads to happier customers and provides very cheap "real time" feedback, so important in a fast-changing world.

There are still a number of reasons that consumers are unwilling to shop the Internet. According to a 1998 Ernst & Young survey, the five key reasons consumers give as to why they haven't bought on-line are shown in Figure 8.7.

As people get comfortable with advances in financial security resulting from improvements in encryption technology, Internet sales will likely skyrocket.

**FIGURE 8.6**

**Products Researched on the Internet but Purchased Through Other Means.***

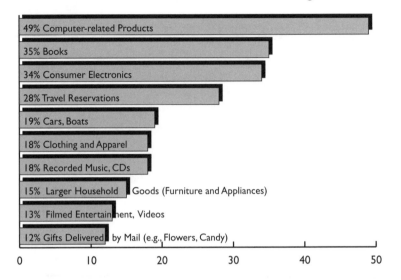

*Percentage of on-line buyers researching each product category on-line then purchasing elsewhere

**FIGURE 8.7**

**Reasons People Will Not Shop On-line**

Percent of Non-Buyers Who Mentioned

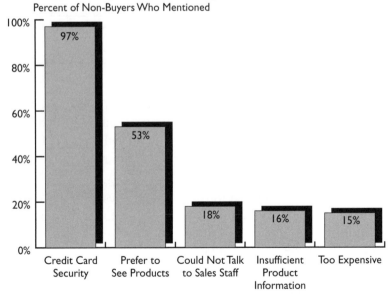

Source: Ernst & Young Survey; Jupiter Communications

## But Is the Internet for Everyone?

Jumping on the Internet is an expensive proposition. International Data Group estimates that the average cost of building an e-commerce site is $6 million and annual maintenance and promotion costs can add another $13 million annually. In the U.S., according to a Deloitte & Touche survey of the Top 100 Retailers, 87 currently have a Web site. In Canada, according to Ernst & Young in their 1998 Retail IT Survey, 69% of Canadian retailers have a Web site, and a further 25% plan to have one within 12 months. This means that by the millennium, fully 94% of Canadian retailers will have a Web site. But only 41% of Canadian retailers sell, or plan to sell, their products on the Internet. The standard excuse given is that "our products won't sell on the Internet." Before making this risky assumption, take a look at Figure 8.8, which outlines the categories of product and services currently selling on-line.

Dell Computer is already selling $10 million worth of computers every day on the Web. Internet retailing will impact many

**FIGURE 8.8**

### % of Purchased Goods by Category Sold On-line (1998)

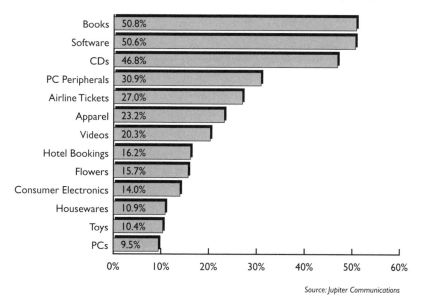

*Source: Jupiter Communications*

**AN INSIDE LOOK**

# SCHWAB—THE POWER OF CHANGE

In late 1997, Charles Schwab & Co. faced a key decision. Based in San Francisco, with revenues of more than $2.5 billion, Schwab pioneered the discount brokerage business. In 1997, the company was America's leading discount brokerage, but was charging commissions that were significantly higher than those of some of its on-line competitors. As lower-priced Internet trading took off, many established players would have tried to buck the trend and maintain margins at the expense of market share. But Charles Schwab embraced change even when the change was difficult.

In January 1998, Schwab cut commissions by more than half, to $29.95 per trade. While the market's immediate reaction was to wipe $125 million off the value of Schwab's stock, the bold change paid off in the long term. Schwab's assets grew 32% in 1998 to $461 billion. The company's shares tripled in the last four months of 1998, pushing the market capitalization to $47 billion, more than that enjoyed by brokerage giant Merrill Lynch, though Merrill Lynch has 13 times the revenue.

Schwab's market share is now three times larger than its next largest on-line trading competitor. And the timing could not be better. On-line accounts are predicted to grow from 6.4 million in 1998 to more than 24.7 million in the U.S. by 2002. With its December 1998 acquisition of the Toronto-based Priority Brokerage Inc., Schwab has now entered the Canadian market.

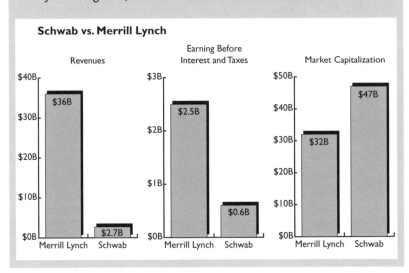

**Schwab vs. Merrill Lynch**

Schwab's Web site averages 33 million hits a day, executing an average of 153,000 trades daily. In the fourth quarter of 1998, fully 60% of Schwab's trades were done on-line, compared to 41% in the same quarter a year earlier – an outcome that clearly exemplifies the power of embracing change. As Co-CEO David Pottruck said in Leonard L. Berry's *Discovering the Soul of Service* (Free Press: 1999), "If our Internet business cannibalizes our other business, at least it is ours."

sectors of traditional retailing. As much as 25% of car retailing will be done on the Web as consumers avoid the hassle of haggling with their local car dealership. Travel agencies will similarly see their world turned upside down. Currently airlines give travel agents an 8% commission, while Internet travel sites receive 5%. The combination of convenience, price, and selection will drive consumers to the Web for their travel purchases and force many travel agencies to the wall.

### Why Jump on the Net When Everyone Is Losing Money?

For all the talk of success on the Net, the reality is that very few sites account for most of the sales, as shown in Figure 8.9.

FIGURE 8.9

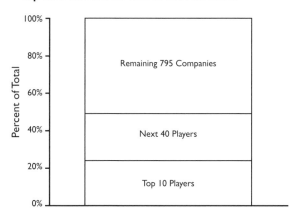

**Top sites account for 76% of Internet Sales**

Forrester Research estimates that as of 1998 only one-third of Web sites are profitable. Many sites are losing money, and several are losing hundreds of millions of dollars every year.

A 1998 Ernst & Young survey on Internet retailer profitability, shown in Figure 8.10, tells a similar story.

**FIGURE 8.10**

**"When do you Expect your Internet Site to be Profitable?"**

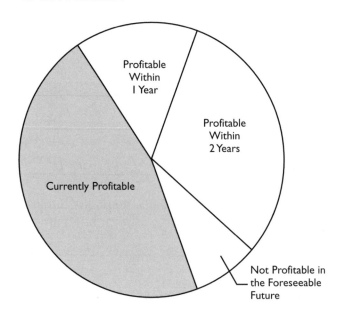

*Source: 1998 Ernst & Young Survey*

## When Will Net Sites Become Profitable?

The red ink will not flow forever. Given the excitement and the explosive growth of the Internet, everyone is jumping onboard, and the capital markets are funnelling billions into this new medium. Three related events will change the current dynamic and lead to a path of profitability:

1. As more and more consumers shop on-line, e-commerce sites will achieve profitable scale.
2. The capital markets will eventually demand profits as opposed to just revenues and this will constrain capital availability.
3. This capital constraint will lead to a shakeout so that fewer players are chasing each product category. Marketing expenses will plateau and prices will stabilize so that the survivors in each sector can earn a respectable return on their investments. This high entry barrier will provide the survivors with sustainable profitability.

However, profits will be held in check by two forces for Internet retailers. First, thanks to shopping agents and general product availability, the consumer will reign supreme and continue to demand the best prices possible, especially for commodity products. Second, the virtual landlords like AOL and Yahoo who "own the eyeballs" (just as Cambridge and Cadillac Fairview own the footsteps in the bricks-and-mortar world) will demand significant virtual rent.

The winners will be the low-cost Internet retailers. Retailers who play in both the bricks-and-mortar world and the virtual world have the potential to be the low-cost provider for three reasons:

1. Brand sharing
2. Sharing of the back-end logistics function
3. Sharing of numerous operational expenses

**1. Brand Sharing**

The Gap already benefits from the worldwide image of the Gap brand. Every Gap ad can be, and is, an ad for Gap.com, and vice versa. The stores themselves are ads for the Web site. JCrew.com is highlighted on receipts in the store and throughout the stores themselves. Given its 520 book superstores, every U.S. book lover knows that barnesandnoble.com is a book site. These stores will become more and more important as the Internet shopping consumer moves from early adapters to more mainstream customers. As a result of this brand/customer sharing, multichannel retailers like The Gap spend significantly less on their Web marketing and advertising as a percentage of revenue, as shown in Figure 8.11.

**FIGURE 8.11**

### Marketing Costs
Marketing costs are much lower for multichannel retailers.

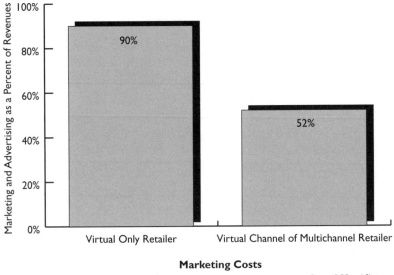

**Marketing Costs**

*Source: BCG and Shop.org*

This base knowledge of the multichannel retailer's brand on the Web provides several advantages beyond just marketing spending. Given that their customers know their brand and the goods they carry, multichannel retailers have much better buyer conversion rates (percentage of people who visit and then buy on the site), as shown in Figure 8.12, and their customers are more loyal, as seen by the repeat buyer percentage in Figure 8.13.

This brand power also results in less dependence on the powerful and very expensive portals for customer traffic for multichannel retailers, as seen in Figure 8.14.

## FIGURE 8.12

### Buyer Conversion Rate

Multichannel retailers have doubled the buyer conversion rates
(percentage of visitors who actually make a purchase).

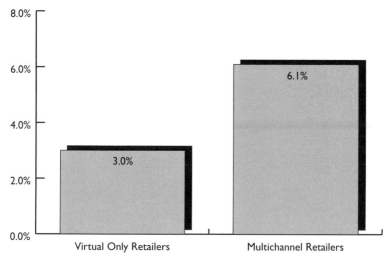

*Source: Shop.org Survey, 11/98*

## FIGURE 8.13

### Repeat Buyers

Multichannel retailers have more repeat buyers.

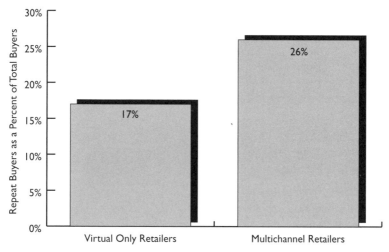

*Source: Shop.org Survey, 11/98*

**FIGURE 8.14**

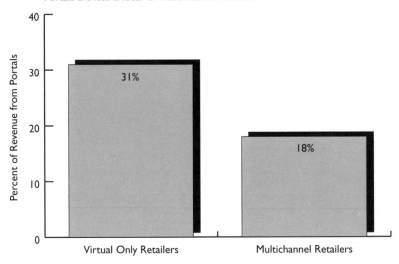

**Importance of Portals**

Portals are less critical for multichannel retailers.

*Source: Shop.org Survey, 11/98*

### 2. Sharing of the Back-End Logistics Function

Virtual-only retailers initially claimed that they had no need for fulfillment capabilities. Wholesalers or suppliers would ship direct to customers thus allowing these new entrants to compete with virtual inventory. The markets loved this world of no costs and unlimited inventory turns. But this phase was short-lived. The combination of increasing customer demand for quicker and more reliable one-stop fulfillment, and the need to cut out mid-dlemen, to increase the virtual retailer's gross margin, has led to many of these original entrants getting into the distribution business. Even Amazon.com has had to build numerous distribution facilities which is driving down its inventory turns and adding tremendous fixed costs to its operations. Once virtual retailers add these fulfillment costs, they are at a

*Retailers who play in both the bricks-and-mortar world and the virtual world benefit from sharing costs, skills, and customers among their channels.*

substantial cost disadvantage versus multichannel retailers. Multi-channel retailers already have these fulfillment capabilities for their own stores and thus Internet fulfillment is a much lower cost option for them than for virtual-only retailers.

Consider the case of Chapters. Chapters has a 306,000-square-foot distribution centre in Brampton, Ontario, to service its 325 retail stores. This is the third-largest distribution centre in North America and carries close to 500,000 individual book titles (by way of comparison, the next largest book distribution centre in Canada carries 5,000 titles). The annual operating costs for this facility are in excess of $10 million. This represents more than four times the entire Internet revenue Chapters had in 1998. Obviously Chapters could not provide its on-line customers with 48-hour access to these 500,000 titles if it were not sharing the annual operating costs of this facility with its bricks-and-mortar business.

### 3. Sharing of Numerous Operational Expenses

Multichannel retailers also share many other costs with their bricks-and-mortar stores. A few areas of sharing include:

- Leveraging buying relationships. WalMart.com gets the buying leverage of the largest retailer in the world. EddieBauer.com already is sending buyers around the world for its catalogue business and they can provide the same world-class products for the Internet site.
- Leveraging technology. The core of Internet technology can be applied to in-store kiosks as a number of retailers are doing. Chapters.ca and the Chapters stores share the same book database, which is extremely complex and expensive to keep current and accurate.
- Leveraging ad copy. Many aspects of the landsend.com Web site are taken directly from the Lands' End catalogue.

At the end of the day, multichannel retailers will triumph. In a few product categories, the bricks-and-mortar market leaders have been slow to respond to the Internet phenomenon, but this will change quickly as these retailers understand the potential of the Internet. Shared skills, shared costs, and shared customers provide multichannel retailers with an insurmountable edge if they do not allow a virtual-only competitor to have a head start. Virtual-only retailers, such as Amazon.com, who had enough of a head start, will do well, but they will be the exception to the rule.

The Net will fundamentally alter the way competition occurs in retailing. In the world of bricks-and-mortar, retailing competition was determined by geography. The Internet has changed all that. The Internet's market is currently global but distribution economics will make the Internet a national business for those businesses that need to ship physical product. Where digital bits are the product, as with music, the Internet may very well be a global business.

## Summary

Power retailers embrace change. The retailers who successfully adapt to the Internet will prove that they understand the fourth principle of successful retailing – the ability to change constantly. As Ed Harsant, President of Staples/Business Depot says, "Retail winners are constantly reinventing their retail strategy, having fun at it, and making a lot of money."

The Internet represents the fastest change that the retail industry has faced this century. Previous shifts were evolutionary as formats changed or were driven by real estate shifts. These previous shifts took time to spread geographically and thus were spaced over decades. The Internet has fundamentally altered retail in less than five years and five years from now will touch every retail format in some way. Now more than ever, retailers will need to master the art of reinventing themselves. Retailers who follow the six steps for successful change outlined in this chapter will position themselves well for the future.

Those retailers who change with the Internet, and who adapt to the other forces facing them, will endure. As Peter Vanexan, the President of Grand & Toy, states, "Lots of people can do well in retail for a year or two, but real retail winners do it year after year – they're durable." They are durable of course, because they constantly change.

# The Chapters Change Epic

Chapters is an enterprise that was born of change itself, the product of a merger between the two largest chains of booksellers in Canada, SmithBooks and Coles. The merger was accompanied by all the attendant traumas of most sea-change situations: layoffs, new bosses, new job descriptions, a new company culture. As Sarah Strachan, who had been VP Operations at Coles before the merger, and is now Senior Vice-President of Mall Stores at Chapters, stated, "The merger was probably the most traumatic event that the companies faced in their forty years of being in business. The pace of change and the new expectations were staggering."

Over the initial four-year period, Chapters underwent a second, even more complex period of change, transforming what was basically a mall-based chain of bookstores into a destination-driven large bookstore business. It is one thing to change; it is another to do so successfully. During its dramatic beginning, Chapters opened a series of large-format stores that became the flagships of the burgeoning chain, which rapidly came to represent over 50% of the company's revenue. At the same time the mall stores improved their profitability, measured as a percentage of sales. After successfully merging, Chapters went on to develop a brand-new kind of venue that proved more successful than the businesses it had inherited four years earlier.

A third major change confronts Chapters heading into the new millennium: that of expansion of its operations onto the Internet. In an auspicious beginning, Chapters was presented with the award for Best Web Site of 1998 in Canada by Internet World. As Rick Segal, President of Chapters Internet, claims, "The Internet will fundamentally change everything in retail."

## The Problem of Resistance

While some degree of turbulence is inevitable in business as in anything else, Chapters' management approaches transition-making as an art – one that requires flexibility, lucid and analytical thinking, and an unflagging will to action.

During the merger and with the building of the larger format stores, there were those who were quick to voice why such plans wouldn't fly, insisting they were out of sync with industry needs. Sceptics abounded. In many cases responses were emotional, not reasoned. The new ideas conjured the arrival of unfamiliar situations, which ran counter to peoples' experiences and set expectations. These visionary ideas evoked fearful responses because they required everyone to gallop into unknown territory.

Some were prepared to go willingly. Others were prepared to leave, and did in fact. Others said they were prepared to stay with the new regime, but dragged their feet. Many of the people running the small bookstores resisted the concept of large bookstores. Many today face the Internet with the same reticence. There is always resistance to change, and Chapters has faced it throughout its growth.

## *Six Keys to Successful Transition*

Chapters has found six ways of making the process of change less unsettling for each of the players in the company. It is through these methods that Chapters continually bridges the gap between the present and the envisioned future.

## 1. Place Value on Communication

Communication is the number-one tool for keeping everyone onside as changes loom on the horizon. Close communication with management and employees from top to bottom is a priority in preserving, and improving upon, the company culture.

Chapters' management invested heavily at the time of the merger on producing a video that carefully explained all the hard facts and their implications. The video was sent to every store from coast to coast. Management and staff were encouraged to screen it, and use it as a basis for discussion and debate.

Chapters has made a point of arranging meetings with individual staff from coast to coast whenever big changes are pending. The face-to-face, personal approach to management-employee relations is basic to the Chapters philosophy. Management devotes far more time than most companies in arranging what it calls "town hall meetings," in which staff are encouraged to ask management questions face to face and obtain immediate replies.

## 2. Align Performance and Rewards

Some companies use entirely seniority-based compensation. If an employee remains there for one more year, he or she is paid a bit more, regardless of the quality of performance. This approach had been used by one of the original companies in the Chapters merger. But then, what if the new company wants to turn left, and the employee insists on going right? Situations arise in which criteria for employee success need to change, too.

When Chapters changed the directions of its two acquired companies, it decided to tie compensation directly to performance. Under the new system, each individual in the entire company was given a performance evaluation. All salary increases – ranging from zero to hefty – now depended on merit and performance. As Mary-Alice Schmidt, Director of Human Resources for Chapters Large-Format Stores, emphasizes, "The merit-driven compensation scheme allows us to reward our best people and serves to put the right incentives in place for the many positive changes we are making."

A bonus scheme was added that included every employee in the company. Even part-time employees can profit, in that if a store was able to achieve its profit target in the quarter and the full year, they also shared in the bonus. While Chapters was stating that it was moving to a new culture, it also made it clear that everyone had the opportunity to share in the success.

## 3. Get the Right People Quickly

A new direction often requires new staff. Chapters management found that once the decisions on direction had been made, new people needed to be hired quickly and without deliberation. They needed to have two qualities: an attitude accepting of the new direction, and the right set of skills.

New hires do not only fill new positions; they can fill new expectations as well. A company's direction can rarely be changed without this infusion of new blood.

By Chapters' fourth year of operation, 70% of the company's top 150 people had been brought in after the merger. Similarly, 80% of the executive team – the Vice Presidents and above – were new to the company. The predecessors of the merger that remained on the Chapters staff were those who possessed the two main qualities that the new management had required in the first place: a positive and flexible attitude, and the right skills.

## 4. Celebrate Often

Employees in uncharted territory are always happy to receive reassurances that the organization is headed in the right direction. No one likes to wander through the woods feeling lost. Celebrating wins, even small ones, is encouraging to everyone, and helps to convert an initial feeling of fragmentation into one of solidarity.

Chapters used a particularly aggressive means of celebrating its merger with yet another aggressive move: it built its first two large-format stores directly after the merger. One was erected in Burnaby, B.C., and the other nearly three thousand miles away in Burlington, Ontario. The reasoning was both inventive and purposeful.

Building in the east and in the west at the same time served to unite the Chapters organization from coast to coast. It gave Chapters staff and customers something to celebrate – at the new stores themselves, and at all the sites in between. The two stores held lavish celebrations. Peter Newman, the celebrated Canadian author, was a guest speaker at the Burnaby opening. But more importantly, everyone in the organization throughout Canada felt part of this growing enterprise.

Company-sponsored gatherings help celebrate wins and bond team members. Broomball games, followed by a social gathering, and baseball barbecues are deemed important for fostering team spirit on a regional level, and also among support office staff. Quarterly meetings are organized that involve the complete support office, while town hall meetings are held every year in cities and towns from coast to coast. Gatherings hosting Chapters' top performers are held often. Ten individuals are selected each year as recipients of the "President's List Award." These superstars are given 1,000 Chapters options and a beautiful Chapters watch designed by Birks. The winners are feted at a special dinner in Toronto annually. As Chris Matichuk, a 1998 President's List winner, says,

"Being selected was an honour for me and all of my team members from my Edmonton store who really deserved this award as much as I did." The company has found that celebrating its successes leads to greater solidarity, while maintaining the momentum of a change initiative; and that taking the time to look back, and celebrating the changes that have been made, help propel the company forward.

## 5. Share the Upside

Change can't happen if there is nothing in it for the employees. Staff are not working to make shareholders happy; they're working to earn a living. Employees are the ones who are making the difficult changes, and they deserve to share in the upside.

Chapters has instituted a number of programs to reward employees who contribute to its overall success. A stock option program ensures that the top 500 individuals will make gains along with Chapters shareholders. In another profit-sharing initiative, as the company makes the right decisions and goes through the accompanying changes, everyone – including part-time booksellers – receive bonuses on both a quarterly and annual basis. An added employee stock ownership plan allows staff to buy stock at a 15% discount through payroll deductions. As Sheila Ahi from the Support Office says, "I own over 400 Chapters shares and, based on my performance, can earn stock options each year. I care about how we do as a company and it's very important to know that we can share in the upside for our contribution to Chapters success."

When employees ask, "What's in it for me?" there needs to be an answer. Chapters has found a number of answers to that important question.

## 6. Institute Feedback Loops

Feedback loops are ways of informing management of changes that are needed. Continuous change particularly requires feedback loops, to make sure that plans are on track. Feedback loops enable staff at all levels in the organization to give responses and make suggestions regarding the changes at hand.

What is a feedback loop? A smoke detector is a simple example. When there's smoke in your house, an alarm bell goes off, telling you to put out the fire. Good companies have strong built-in feedback loops, not just to sound an alarm, but to plan ahead and make changes so that alarms will not be necessary.

Chapters focuses on three key feedback loops: (1) customer research/ retention, (2) employee feedback and (3) financial and competitor monitoring. Chapters uses feedback loops extensively to monitor conditions within their stores, and the industry itself. By monitoring the successes of a competitor's store in comparison to one of their own, or of a competitor's promotion that earned them an especially good fiscal week, Chapters can consider future changes they might make for their own benefit. By measuring the retention rates of their own loyalty programs, the company can determine performance right down to store level. How does this help the organization? If all other stores have an 80% retention rate, and a certain store has only a 60% retention of its loyalty card members, the alarm is sounded for needed improvement in the store that is underperforming.

Chapters has found company-wide climate surveys and upward feedback forms indispensable in gauging appropriateness of actions taken, and the feelings people have about changes that are either forthcoming or in midstream. Use of these feedback loops allows everyone to speak their personal truths, rather than spouting what others might want to hear.

Finally, feedback loops that gauge financial performance are used to benchmark the company against all other booksellers worldwide, on whom Chapters has a financial profile. Chapters checks its own financial dimensions against those of its competitors, in areas as specific as sales per square foot, profit margins, and labour costs. If a competitor is stronger in certain areas, then Chapters management looks for the reasons for the differences. Keeping track of the positives and negatives of change in relation to the competition is imperative.

Following these six keys has allowed Chapters to successfully accomplish three transitions in the past four years. The first successful transition was the original 1995 merger. The second was the launch of book superstores and the transformation from a mall-based business to a destination store business. The third transition has just begun as Chapters launches itself full steam onto the Internet.

# 9 Wal-Mart– The World's Leading Retailer

> *"There are other companies that are good at certain segments of retailing but there is no one that does it as well across the board as Wal-Mart. They don't have any weak links."*
>
> – Don Spindel, analyst, A.G. Edwards, quoted in *Fortune*

Rather than just summarizing the previous eight chapters, we chose to highlight one great retailer who consistently applies our four rules for retail success. Many great retailers could have been chosen such as Home Depot, or The Gap, or Canada's own Loblaw. Our survey of retail CEOs asked retailers to list the retail companies they watch most closely to get new ideas from. As shown in Figure 9.1, Wal-Mart outpaced all 106 retailers mentioned by fellow CEOs. The top five retailers mentioned were Wal-Mart, Loblaws, Home Depot, Chapters, and Sears Canada.

Wal-Mart is an excellent retailer to use to integrate our findings because its track record of success is the longest and because it has applied our four rules to a very mature sector – discount department stores. Sam Walton built his first Wal-Mart in Rogers, Arkansas, in 1962 and in the space of just three decades Wal-Mart became the largest retailer in the world. For the second year in a row, as seen in Figure 9.2, Wal-Mart was the most admired general merchandiser in the U.S. according to *Fortune*'s ranking.

FIGURE 9.1

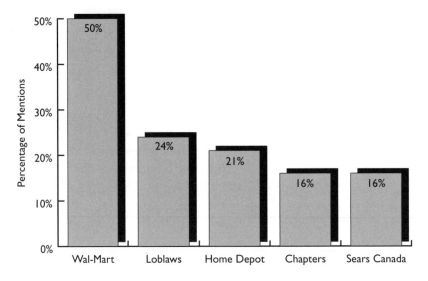

### Retail Companies You Watch Most Closely for Ideas
Wal-Mart is the most watched for ideas by retail CEOs.

*Source: Retail CEO Survey (October 1998)*

FIGURE 9.2

**General Merchandisers – 1998 *Fortune* Most Admired Companies**

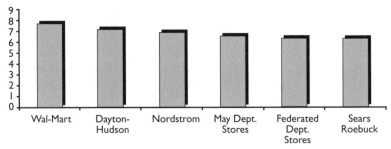

Wal-Mart now employs over 900,000 associates in its more than 3,600 stores worldwide. It created some 105,000 new jobs in the last two years alone.

One need only look at Wal-Mart's financial track record in Figures 9.3 and 9.4 to see how it has outpaced its key direct competitor, K-Mart.

**FIGURE 9.3**

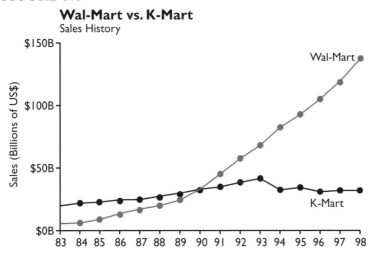

**Wal-Mart vs. K-Mart**
Sales History

**FIGURE 9.4**

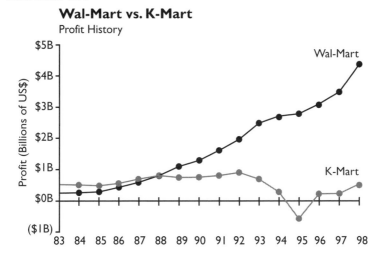

**Wal-Mart vs. K-Mart**
Profit History

Wal-Mart's profit margins almost triple K-Mart's and it tracks at a P/E (price/earning ratio) of 49 compared to K-Mart's 18. Wal-Mart's arrival in Canada literally changed retailing in Canada forever with lower prices. As David Brodie, Wood Gundy's retail analyst, says, "What did Wal-Mart mean to Canada? It meant: Get smart, or pack up your bags." Consumers benefited but the increased competition pushed some retailers like Consumers Distributing and Eaton's to the wall. Wal-Mart's intense pressure on prices helped drive Zellers' EBIT (earnings before interest and taxes) margins from just under 6% in 1994 to less than 1% in 1996 and prompted the distant number-three player in the discount department store sector, K-Mart, to pull out of Canada by selling to The Bay.

Figure 9.5 shows how the Canadian discount department store shares changed between 1994 and 1998.

**FIGURE 9.5**

**Canadian Department Store Share Percentage of Total**

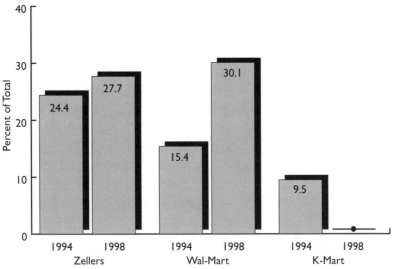

The success of Wal-Mart Canada is clear looking at the key metric of sales per square foot, as shown in Figure 9.6, versus its key competitor, Zellers, since it took over Woolco in 1994.

Wal-Mart, the world's largest, and arguably the world's best all-around retailer, with $137 billion in sales in 1998, epitomizes the rules of "Power Retailers." The Wal-Mart formula parallels the rules for success we have articulated.

**FIGURE 9.6**

## Discount Department Stores Sales Per Square Foot

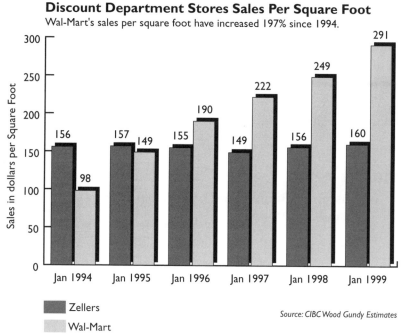

Wal-Mart's sales per square foot have increased 197% since 1994.

Source: CIBC Wood Gundy Estimates

## Principle I – A Compelling RVP

Wal-Mart will not be undersold. It has established a unique and sustainable position with its core customers which revolves around the key criterion of price. As Thomas Coughlin, President of Wal-Mart's Discount Stores Division in the U.S., says, "Our retail philosophy rests perhaps more than any other retailer on the value-price relationship. It's incumbent on us to always have the best value for our customers." Wal-Mart may not have the widest selection or the most awesome customer service – and the cavernous stores don't exactly conjure convenience – but loyal customers are back week after week to get the best prices in town. In the U.S., Wal-Mart shoppers spend on average two and a half times more per annum than the average K-Mart shopper. As one of their competitors, Paul Walters of Sears Canada, recently said in *Maclean's*, "I think Wal-Mart is just another example of a company that is more focused on its customers."

One need only look at the 1998 *Major Market Retail Report* by Kubas Consultants to see that Wal-Mart was ranked number one of all the department stores in value for money, as shown in Figure 9.7.

This gap in customer perception of value is incredible. Nine points separate Wal-Mart from the next best competitor. Only

**FIGURE 9.7**

### Customer Ranking out of Possible 100 on "Value for Money"

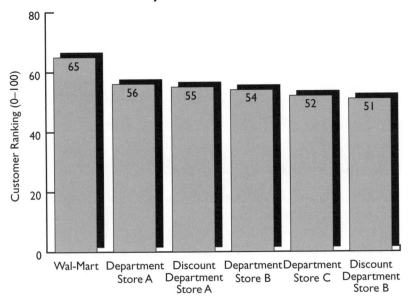

Source: 1998 MMRR/Kubas Consultants

five points separate the other five Canadian department store competitors. This performance gap on the key price dimension of RVP means that customers are more loyal to Wal-Mart, shop it more often, and buy more when they are there. A lethal and winning combination. As Dave Ferguson, President and CEO of Wal-Mart Canada, states, "Our pricing is fluid as we are constantly striving to have the best price." When Wal-Mart enters a new market, it will not be undersold. A Queen's University study done in 1995 in Kingston confirms Wal-Mart's performance on this price dimension. The study looked at six department store competitors in the Kingston area. Just one year after coming to Kingston, Wal-Mart had tripled its share

> *Wal-Mart will not be undersold, and its customers' strong perception of its winning RVP means that they are more loyal to Wal-Mart, shop there more often, and buy more when they are there.*

of primary shoppers to 22% from 7%. How? Price. Asked which stores had the lowest prices, Kingston shoppers rated Wal-Mart top of the six as fully 44% said Wal-Mart had the lowest prices compared to 37% who mentioned Zellers and 7% who said K-Mart. All this was accomplished in one short year.

Everything Wal-Mart does is tied to achieving superiority on this critical dimension of RVP. Its strategy and organization are perfectly aligned with delivering this value proposition every day. This value gap means that Wal-Mart is the preferred retailer for shoppers in most of its product categories, as shown in Figure 9.8. In a study done in three U.S. cities in 1993, Wal-Mart was one of the top three choices for consumers in 36 out of 43 product categories. K-Mart was in the top three in only 10, despite having more stores in the three studied markets than Wal-Mart (87 K-Mart stores to Wal-Mart's 68 stores).

## Principle 2 – Achieve Leadership Position in Geographic Markets, Categories, and Channels

Today, Wal-Mart is the largest retailer in the world, but thirty years ago it was largely unknown outside of Bentonville, Arkansas. Today Wal-Mart dominates its product and customer segments in every geographic market in which it chooses to compete. This was also true thirty years ago. All that changed was the geographic scope of Wal-Mart. In the beginning, Wal-Mart chose small towns which it could dominate with its large well-run discount department stores. It then spread methodically in concentric circles in a classic execution of a retail cluster strategy.

Wal-Mart understands the value of dominant position. Even back in 1987 when it was smaller than K-Mart in absolute size and in national market share, it was already the market leader in those markets in which it chose to compete. Thus, as shown in Figure 9.9, Wal-Mart achieved a higher return on assets than did its direct

**FIGURE 9.8**

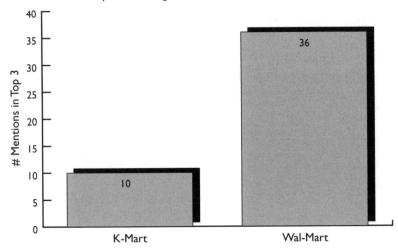

### Wal-Mart's Customer Franchise
Wal-Mart is one of the Top 3 preferred retailers for consumers in 36 out of 43 product categories.

*Source: Tigert Study of 3 U.S. Cities (March '93)*

**FIGURE 9.9**

### Share of Top 50 SMSAs vs. Profitability
Discount Department Store (FY 1984–1987)

Source: *Annual Reports, Chain Store Guide*

discount department store competitors. Scale in target markets helped drive superior profit performance.

The dominant market position allows Wal-Mart to:

- use its distribution facilities efficiently
- leverage spending on regional advertising
- hire the best local talent
- improve buying terms to pass savings on to customers
- take advantage of operational economies thanks to its cluster strategy.

## Principle 3 – Execute Better than Competitors on the Areas of People, Technology, and Costs

### People

Dave Ferguson summed it up this way, "I think good leadership holds people accountable. Generally what we find is that eight other people suffer when one partner fails to deliver. I owe it to the eight others, not the one." Wal-Mart holds people accountable.

Wal-Mart has a strong culture which emphasizes that local staff who have the contact with customers drive the whole enterprise. These folks in the front lines know what is actually going on and thus the senior staff in Bentonville listen to their people. As George Stalk of the Boston Consulting Group stated in his 1992 *Harvard Business Review* article on Wal-Mart: "The job of senior management at Wal-Mart is not to tell individual store managers what to do, but to create an environment where they can learn from the market and from each other." As Dave Ferguson added, "We have a concept based on ownership at every job level. It's the major ingredient as to why it works. We provide an environment and a culture that is grass-roots driven. We listen to those internal customers at our weekly meetings." Central to the Wal-Mart culture is the fact that senior managers lead from the front. They are hard-working (including Saturday mornings) and "walk the walk and talk the talk." As Sam himself said, "I can't see asking our folks in the stores to make the sacrifice while our managers are off playing golf on Saturday mornings."

The key is that Wal-Mart staff are capable and motivated. As Dave Ferguson pointed out:

"I support the store staff because they are on the firing line. We want everyone in the company to believe they are an agent of the customer. When we have a culture like that, people do extraordinary things." Wal-Mart staff have the information and authority to make the right decisions for their customers. As Sam Walton, Wal-Mart's founder, claimed in his autobiography, *Sam Walton: Made in America: My Story* (Bantam Books, 1993):

> Another important ingredient from the very beginning has been our very unusual willingness to share most of the numbers of our business with all the associates. It's the only way they can possibly do their job to the best of their abilities. We were among the first in our industry with the idea of

empowering our associates by running the business practically as an open book. We share with them their store's profits, their store's purchases, their store's sales, and their store's markdowns. We share that information with every part-time employee in the stores.

They are on a winning team and through bonuses and profit sharing, Wal-Mart employees share in Wal-Mart's success. To quote Sam Walton again:

The more you share profits with your associates, the more profit will accrue to the company. Why? Because the way management treats the associate is exactly how the associates will then treat the customers. And if the associates treat the customers well, the customer will return again and again and that is where the real profit in this business lies. Satisfied, loyal, repeat customers are at the heart of Wal-Mart's spectacular profit margins, and those customers are loyal to us because our associates treat them better than salespeople in other stores do.

Thanks to profit sharing and employee share ownership plans, many associates are sitting on nest eggs worth more than $200,000. Wal-Mart's "people focus" led to its being selected by *Fortune* as one of the 100 best companies to work for in the U.S. in 1998.

## ▉ *Technology*

Wal-Mart has invested in excess of $1 billion building the largest civilian database of its kind in the world (bigger even than AT&T's). As Dave Ferguson states, "You have to be on the front edge in terms of supporting your people with information." Some 90% of Wal-Mart's software is written in-house by some 1,000 full-time developers. Despite having developed technology as a core competency, Wal-Mart can spend less on technology (0.5% of sales compared to 1.4% for the industry) thanks to scale. Technology allows stores to communicate to Bentonville and Bentonville to communicate to the stores effectively through a sophisticated satellite network.

Through its "Retail Link" computer system, Wal-Mart tracks virtually every item. This means that Wal-Mart can have the right product in the right place at the right time. This enables Wal-Mart to vary inventory by individual store and by season of the year. The result is less stock-outs and the ability to carry the products customers want in their neighbourhood Wal-Mart store. Wal-Mart understands that technology is the core nervous system for any successful retailer. As Sanford C. Bernstein analyst Ursula Moran states, "Their information systems are in a class apart – really ahead of any other retailer I know."

## ■ Costs

Somehow Wal-Mart manages to charge lower prices to its customers and yet still make more profit than its competitors. How does it weave this magic? By aggressively managing its costs. Despite a gross margin which is 2 to 3% lower than competitors' (because of lower prices), Wal-Mart ends up making a return on assets that is double that of its competitors. The cost advantage starts with tough buying. Procter & Gamble sells more to Wal-Mart than it does to all of Japan. This scale gives Wal-Mart tremendous leverage, which they use to get the lowest possible prices for their customers. Beyond buying leverage, Wal-Mart achieves cost efficiency in five primary areas:

1. Because it achieves significantly higher sales per square foot than competitors, Wal-Mart ends up with lower occupancy costs and employee costs per square foot.
2. Wal-Mart has much lower distribution costs thanks to its world-class logistics operation. Wal-Mart puts 85% of its goods through its warehouse system, compared to K-Mart's 50%. This allows it to be in-stock, have a 50% better inventory turn than K-Mart,

and gives it a full 1% of sales cost advantage over its competitors. It costs Wal-Mart 3 to 4% to ship goods to stores, compared to competitors' costs of from 4.5 to 5%.

3. Because satisfied customers keep coming back, Wal-Mart can advertise less than competitors. A number of department store competitors spend 3 to 4% of sales on advertising. K-Mart spends 1.7% of sales and yet Wal-Mart spends less than 0.5% of sales on advertising.

4. Thanks to a motivated staff who share in a bonus for hitting shrink targets, Wal-Mart is able to save fully 1% of sales on shrink compared to competitors. The greeters also play a subtle role in reducing shrink by letting people know they have been acknowledged coming into the store.

5. Wal-Mart watches its overhead pennies carefully. As *Business Week* noted, "Visitors to Bentonville often mistake Wal-Mart's office building, with its lobby decorated in Early Bus Station, for a warehouse." Wal-Mart's overhead as a percentage of sales is a full half point lower than competitors.

**FIGURE 9.10**

### Wal-Mart's Cost Advantage
Wal-Mart enjoys a full 7.5% cost advantage versus competitors

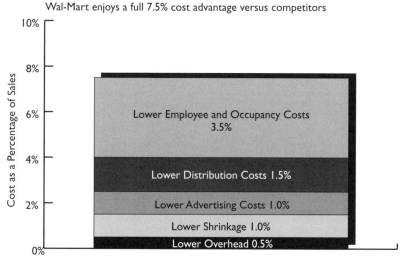

Thus, as seen in Figure 9.10, Wal-Mart has a 7.5% cost advantage versus its competitors and it chooses to pass 5% of this along to customers in price savings, keeping 2.5% for itself in additional profits. Lest anyone believe that this 5% savings for customers is bogus, remember that numerous studies have shown that the prices for similar baskets of goods fell 6 to 8% in the two years after Wal-Mart's entry into Canada. As Sam Walton said in his autobiography, "Control your expenses better than your competition. This is where you can always find the competitive advantage. For 25 years running – long before Wal-Mart was known as the nation's largest retailer – we ranked number one in our industry for the lowest ratio of expenses to sales. You can make a lot of different mistakes and still recover if you run an efficient operation."

### Principle 4 – Lead Change

Sam Walton was never ashamed to admit that he learned from his competitors. He copied their best ideas constantly. He was always changing his Wal-Mart formula to better serve customer needs. Post-Sam, Wal-Mart has continued to push the envelope as it has become one of the largest food retailers in the U.S. through its 500 Supercentres. It is also testing a smaller grocery concept called Neighbourhood Markets.

Everyone focuses on Wal-Mart's stunning success but few realize that a large part of that success comes from a culture which welcomes change and which is willing to experiment and try new things. Failure is tolerated as long as people are trying new ideas. Does anyone remember Wal-Mart's foray into discount drugs with Dots or into arts and crafts with Helen's Arts and Crafts in the early 1980s? Probably not. But by trying new ideas, they ended up with success in groceries and with Sam's Wholesale Clubs. They also incorporated a lot of learning from Dots Drugs into their Wal-Mart stores. Power retailers are always willing to try new ideas.

**FIGURE 9.11**

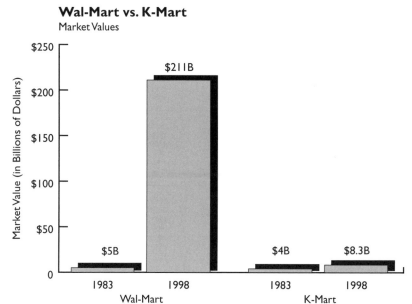

**Wal-Mart vs. K-Mart**
Market Values

## Summary

Wal-Mart has been the outstanding retailer of the past 30 years. In Canada, it has already catapulted itself to the number-one position in the department store sector. In 1999, it will add 17 new stores in Canada and will probably double its sales to $12 billion over the next five years. This number could be significantly higher if it decides to sell groceries as it has done in the U.S. Wal-Mart has changed Canadian retailing forever. The strong will adapt to compete against the best retailer in the world; many others will perish.

Wal-Mart's success has been great for consumers, who enjoy lower prices, and for its employees, who have had tremendous career opportunities as the giant merchandiser experiences double-digit growth. But investors have been rewarded as well. The lucky initial investors who invested $1,000 in Wal-Mart when it went public in the early 1970s would now have stock worth more than $2.7 million. Over the past 16 years, Wal-Mart's market value, as seen in Figure 9.11, has skyrocketed, while its chief competitor, K-Mart, has remained essentially flat.

No retailer has added more Market Value than Wal-Mart. In 1998, Wal-Mart was again the retail leader in business consultant Stern Stewart's MVA (Market Value Added) analysis, with Home Depot in second place and The Gap in third spot.

Wal-Mart and many other retailers are adhering to the four principles we have outlined. We've featured Chapters' as a recurring example for each principle because we had complete access to Chapters data and management as part of our research. Numerous other retailers, including, but not limited to, Home Depot, Loblaws, and The Gap would have been equally relevant case histories. These are all companies that understand their customers, dominate their markets, execute brilliantly, and are constantly willing to change and reinvent themselves. These are the power retailers of the 21st century.

---

## A Retail Winner In Four Years

**THE CHAPTERS' PERSPECTIVE**

Chapters has managed to turn itself into a retail winner within a period of only four years, by acting forcefully upon a solid vision. First, the company purchased the two top bookselling chains in Canada – Coles and SmithBooks – and merged them into one united retail power. The resulting financial strength gave Chapters the ability to invest aggressively in developing two brand new RVPs: a burgeoning chain of large-format stores, which rapidly came to more than double the company's sales, and more recently with the Internet business. To support all of these ventures, Chapters built its own distribution business, to enable optimum delivery of orders and immediate replenishment of stock.

Chapters knew its objective from the start: to become Canada's signature book retailer from coast to coast. To make this happen, it first had to know its potential customers. It identified its book-buying public through a series of market segmentation studies, which grew increasingly distilled and refined until a strong customer profile was at last attained. A general survey revealed that education was a larger driver of book purchases than income, and that the learned remained hungry for knowledge and literary entertainment.

## *A Winning Retail Value Proposition*

Surveys of Chapters customers and non-customers revealed particular preferences for the company's particular venues. What would existing customers and potential customers like to see in Chapters outlets that would sway them to change their shopping preferences? It became clear that, within the newly defined book retail universe, there existed a large gap where a new breed of store could have strong appeal: one that valued the combination of an enormous book selection with discount pricing. Through such detailed strategizing, potential was seen to construct a coast-to-coast chain of large-format bookstores, while nurturing the existing mall stores to greater productivity.

Instead of having one RVP for a single business as is true of most companies, Chapters devised a three-pronged strategy, with an individual RVP for each of its three distinct businesses: the mall stores, with their convenient locations and emphasis on popular titles and authors; the Internet, offering ease of shopping from an unprecedented spectrum of three million titles; and its large-format stores, providing optimum service, selection, and discount prices.

The RVP of the superstores is clearly selection. For three years running (1999, 1998, 1997), Chapters was rated as the top retailer in Canada on selection by customers across Canada. Internal customer market surveys show that 91% of Chapters customers rate Chapters as superior to other bookstores and 9% rate Chapters the same as other bookstores (none rate Chapters inferior to other bookstores). An important value added to the RVP in the superstores was the emotional engagement of customers of all ages. Fun and entertainment were infused throughout the world of books, by creating colourful and interactive children's sections, the Hear Music department, the Active Minds lectures and presentations, and community-wide events featuring music, readings, and public appearances by well-known celebrities.

## *A Clear Path to Market Leadership*

The merger of SmithBooks and Coles instantly gave Chapters by far the largest market share in the Canadian bookselling market, but the addition of the superstores, and more recently the Internet, made the company's leadership unassailable. Chapters national market share, built upon local market leadership, accrued to a $570-million-dollar business for Chapters by 1999. As David Brodie, Retail Analyst at CIBC Wood Gundy, says, "Chapters has achieved a degree of dominance in its industry seldom matched in Canadian retailing."

## *A Commitment to Superior Execution*

Chapters believes that the key to its success is, far above all else, its human capital. People and their relationships are the ties that bind the company together and keep it on the road to success. The booksellers who work the floors are the lifeblood of the organization.

Implicit to this philosophy is the belief that employees are more important than their customers – the rationale being that a truly satisfied staff member is going to be more inclined to happily serve a patron than a disgruntled employee. Sought-after qualities in staff are a positive attitude, a gregarious character, a love of books, and – given Chapters' aggressiveness in meeting new challenges – a readiness to embrace change. Team spirit is especially valued in hopefuls seeking management positions.

A comprehensive range of incentive programs makes employees constantly aware of their importance to the company. Full-time and part-time booksellers receive quarterly and annual bonuses in profit-earning stores. Many top performers have seen their overall compensation increase over 50% in the four years since Chapters was formed, thanks to salary increases, bonus programs, and accelerated promotions for outstanding performance.

To increase its profit margin, Chapters looked for the ways it could significantly reduce costs. By integrating the management of several hundred stores under one roof, Chapters was able to reduce its "above the store" costs by two percentage points. A lowered rent-to-sales ratio increased profits by another one percent, through the closing of small-performance mall stores, and emphasizing the building of new large-format stores. Of the remaining mall bookstores, those that were underperforming were brought up to industry average by benchmarking their labour costs.

Freight costs were also minimized through Chapters' building of its distribution business, which was enabled by the company's size. The in-house supply and distribution system generated constant savings through the shipping of its own product, and will continue to be a significant asset as the large-format stores grow and as the Internet business accelerates.

## *A Willingness to Embrace Change*

Chapters made numerous transitions in its four-year birthing period. The company's very creation was turbulent in itself, having been a merger of Canada's two primary institutions in the Canadian panorama of book-sellers: SmithBooks and Coles. In this initial four-year period, unsuccessful mall stores were shut down, profitable ones were shored up for better performance, the trajectory for a new chain of superstores was established, and another completely new Chapters business began serving customers on the Internet.

Resistance to all these changes was inevitable, since not everyone thrives on the psychological challenges of constant change. But it was only through making these changes that Chapters was able to establish itself as the number-one bookseller in Canada.

All this change led to a company that has had a superlative financial performance. As shown by the chart below, bigger is better, and aggressive, incisive management pays huge dividends.

## Chapters Financial Performance 1995–1999
Fiscal Years ending March

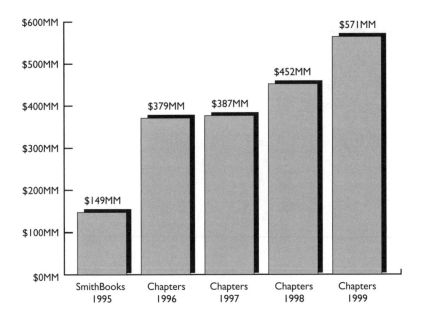

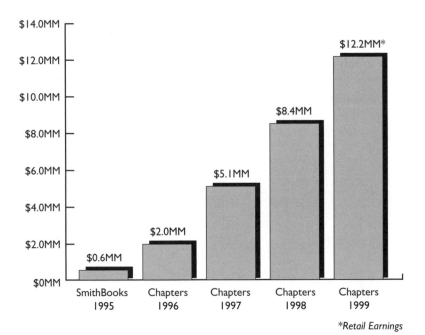

*Retail Earnings*

# ARE YOU A POWER RETAILER?

| PRINCIPLE 1 | PRINCIPLE 2 | PRINCIPLE 3 | PRINCIPLE 4 |
|---|---|---|---|
| *Deliver a customer-driven superior, Retail Value Proposition (RVP).* | *Achieve leadership position in product, geographic, and channel markets.* | *Execute better than competitors on the dimensions of people, costs, and technology.* | *Lead change.* |
| 1) Do you have a clearly identified target customer segment based on its needs and is your organization fully aligned with this segment? | 3) Are you the dominant market leader in your business in the correctly defined geographic market? | 5) Do prospective and current employees rate you as the absolute preferred place to work in your industry? | 9) Do you have financial, customer, and employee feedback loops in place to provide early warning of the need for change? |
| 2) Do you clearly outperform competitors on your chosen RVP based on customer perception? | 4) Are you the market leader in your chosen product categories with relevant channels? | 6) Have you developed leading edge technology to manage your products/stores in a real-time fashion? | 10) Do 20% of today's revenues come from products, channels, or geographic markets that did not exist three years ago? |
| | | 7) Do you have a customer database management system which tracks SKUs and customers together? | |
| | | 8) Have your costs per transaction declined 20% over the past five years? | |

*If you honestly respond yes to at least eight of these 10 questions then you are a qualified "power"*
*retailer. If you answered yes to five or fewer, then you are in a truly "precarious" position.*

# Index